KW-484-167

THIS COULD HAVE BEEN PREVENTED!

I t wasn't until after my second life-threatening crash that helmets were finally issued to the team. Too late for me—I had already tested gravity twice and lost.

For years, people have assumed that my ski crash was just an unfortunate accident—an unlucky twist of fate on the slopes. That's the easy version of the story, the one that makes sense on the surface. But the truth is far more unsettling.

The night before that fateful morning, I had too much to drink. A culture where allegedly, excessive drinking isn't just accepted but expected. A culture where camaraderie is often measured in pints rather than in discipline or responsibility.

At the time, I brushed it off as harmless fun, just another night of unwinding. But looking back, the alarm bells had been ringing long before I got back on my skis. My body felt sluggish, my reactions dulled, my judgment clouded—subtle signs I ignored, convincing myself I was fine. That first crash should have been a wake-up call. Instead, it was met with laughter and a trophy of sorts—a goofy leopard-print chef's hat, awarded for having the "Best Crash of the Day." A joke, a bit of banter, nothing more. Yet in hindsight, it felt more like a cruel omen, a warning disguised as humour.

I was part of that culture. We all were. It was the norm. And it came at a cost.

I don't share this training now to seek sympathy or forgiveness. I share it because my story is not unique. Across the Armed Forces, countless soldiers have met their fate in exercises, adventurous pursuits, and even daily routines—not just because of misfortune or miscalculation, but because they had a carried the weight of the night before. Many of these incidents were avoidable. Many of these lives could have been different.

Yet, we rarely speak of it. It's easier to chalk these accidents up to bad luck or the inherent risks of an active lifestyle. But how many of these so-called 'accidents' had alcohol as their silent

Life Is All About Choices

Victory over Rejection

Alexander Laing

Copyright © 2025 Alexander Laing

All rights reserved. No part of this book may be reproduced, stored, or transmitted by any means—whether auditory, graphic, mechanical, or electronic—without written permission of both publisher and author, except in the case of brief excerpts used in critical articles and reviews. Unauthorized reproduction of any part of this work is illegal and is punishable by law.

accomplice? How many talented, capable soldiers have suffered because the culture told them that restraint was weakness and excess was camaraderie?

I leave this here not as an accusation, but as a truth that needs to be confronted. We pride ourselves on discipline, on excellence, on pushing ourselves beyond limits. But perhaps the bravest thing we can do is ask the uncomfortable question:

Is this the cost we are willing to keep paying?

GRATITUDE

efore I begin, I feel compelled to make a small disclaimer: The Armed Forces, where I once found camaraderie, did not bend to the demands of political correctness. My transparency in recounting these experiences may unsettle the more sensitive souls among you, but I believe in presenting the truth as it was. It is what it is—unyielding, unapologetic, and real.

In 2002, fate led me to cross paths with Graham Peddie, the visionary founder of Pitstop in Leatherhead, Surrey. During our encounter, Graham recognized something in me—a resilience, a spark—and he invited me to give a speech on 'Having a Positive Outlook.' He believed I embodied that sentiment, and it was through this experience that the seeds of my creative writing journey were planted.

I cannot move forward without expressing profound gratitude to my family and friends, who revealed their truest selves through the love and sacrifices they made for me. Theresa Franklin was a guiding light, much like a caring auntie, always encouraging and steadfast in her belief that I could and should write this book. Her unwavering support had been a cornerstone of this journey.

Last year has seen the most noticeable changes to my first edition of this book by Sue and David encouraging me to start with a James Bond style of an introduction.

I dedicate this book in loving memory of my stepmother, Deryth, who embodied the spirit of a fun-loving, industrious lady. She lived with integrity and unshakable character, leaving a legacy that continues to inspire me. Her memory is my 'why.'

INTRODUCTION

The adrenaline surged through my veins, excitement blending with sheer exhilaration as I glided down the piste. The cold mountain air stung my face, and the snow crunched under my skis as I navigated each twist and turn, lost in the thrill that only the slopes could offer. But as I neared the crest of the hill, something shifted inside me. A voice I should have ignored whispered in my mind, urging me to lean back, to defy everything I'd trained for. That was when everything went horribly wrong!

In an instant, I was no longer in control. My skis, once an extension of my body, became a runaway force. The first impact struck like a sledgehammer—knocking me out cold, as though I had just taken a perfect uppercut from a heavyweight boxer. From that moment, I was a ragdoll, tumbling helplessly down the slope, a blur of limbs and skis, with somersaults thrown in for good measure....

This was no ordinary fall. It wasn't something I could laugh off and shake my head at. No, this was something darker, more sinister. I was now at the mercy of Mother Nature, or whatever higher power governs such moments. There was no bargaining with her—only survival.

When I finally came to rest at the foot of the slope, battered and broken, the world around me felt distant and surreal. I was alive, yes, but everything had changed in those few, terrifying seconds. Time seemed to stand still as my ski team scrambled to keep me alive. One teammate stood at the top of the slope, crossing his skis over his head to warn others. The medic ran through the emergency ABCs, while the team captain frantically tried to locate the rescue team, who was nowhere in sight. Jackets were laid all around me to fight off hypothermia, as I began to show signs of freezing.

After what felt like an eternity, a snowmobile carrying the rescue team appeared over the ridge, and I was rushed away from the crash site. The slope was closed off for investigation, the aftermath of my accident rippling through the resort. Meanwhile, my ski captain contacted the regiment back home, and a liaison officer was sent to inform my parents. Saddened and anxious, they packed a suitcase for the next flight out of Heathrow to Oslo.

By the time they arrived, I had been induced into a coma at Lillehammer hospital. My brain needed rest, and I was surrounded by tubes and machines, my body a battlefield of injuries. My parents were met by the ski team, who shared their sorrow, before being taken to a hotel where they stayed for a few days. Then I was transferred to a brain specialist hospital in Oslo, where my parents found hope.

It was the sound of my father's distinct horse mimicking footsteps entering my ward that became the turning point. Even in my unconscious state, something stirred inside me. My right hand lifted from the wrist, as though I was reaching out. Tears filled my parents' eyes—a sign that I was still here, that I was on the road to recovery.

The brain damage I sustained that day was invisible to the naked eye, but it carved deep scars inside me. It robbed me of the life I once knew, leaving me to battle symptoms that lurked in the shadows, waiting to strike whenever I was under pressure or pushed too far. The frontal lobe had taken the brunt of the impact, the part of the brain that shaped so much of who I was. The damage was permanent, and its effects rippled through every facet of my life.

Ten to fifteen years later, ski helmets became mandatory. A policy change that arrived too little, too late—for me. I had fallen outside the window for compensation.

And the officer in charge? He had been wearing a helmet from the very start. He knew the risk. He protected himself of course, because leadership is about ensuring personal safety first....

I could have let bitterness take root. But I refused to let resentment define me. Instead, I now carry a testimony—time truly is the greatest healer, and through it all, I've come to realize that there's more to life than meets the eye.

Although, I still think Forrest Gump said it best: *"Life is like a box of chocolates—you never know what you're gonna get."*

CHAPTER ONE

Greenford

If you could travel back in time, what choices would you reconsider? What paths would you walk differently?

I often wonder if there were moments when Dad regretted introducing me to mini rugby just before my sixth birthday. It was a pivotal moment, one that allowed me to bond with him in the most physical of ways—through unexpected tackles from behind. Supporting your son in mini rugby is like walking a tightrope, balancing between an encouraging parent, and changing into something more formidable, even overbearing.

There was one game where I collided headfirst with another player, the impact sending me to the ground in tears. As I lay there, sobbing, Dad's voice boomed over the field, "It's only pain!" In that instant, I swallowed my tears, got back on my feet, and continued playing, much to the disapproval of the supporting mothers. Some might see this as an example of neglect, a moment to hold against my dad—some spoiled kids might even consider it grounds for a lawsuit. But the truth is, we can never fully grasp the challenges our parents faced until we become parents ourselves. Instead of holding onto resentment, I choose to see it as character-building—a lesson in resilience. As the saying goes, *"what doesn't kill me will only make me stronger."*

My story began at Edgware Hospital on 17th November 1974. The first six months of my life were spent above a shop in Canons Park, Edgware. After that, I was whisked away to our first house with a garden, nestled on Long Drive in Greenford, Middlesex. There, I grew up alongside my dad, Tony; mum, Carol; older sister Joanna; and Toby MKII, our beloved labrador, who had the uncanny ability to clear a room with his farts before making a swift exit, as if he knew exactly what he was doing! Our home was a whirlwind of organized chaos, but amidst the disorder, there was always joy. Mum, bless her, deserved a medal for her incredible multitasking skills.

My parents were the embodiment of hard work and determination, juggling three thriving transport businesses during the 70s and 80s from their rented depot in Shepherd's Bush, West London. They owned Adventurous Haulage of London, Adventurous Coaches of London, and the incredibly busy Adventurous Recovery & Repairs London. The latter held the contract with the Metropolitan Police, responsible for clearing accident scenes and ensuring the roads were safe again.

Dad, ever the strategist, chose the name Adventurous Coaches with an eye toward practicality—it ensured the company appeared early in the Yellow Pages, catching the eye of potential clients before the competition.

The full weight of managing three businesses and raising two mischievous children fell squarely on Mum's shoulders. She faced this overwhelming responsibility with a down-to-earth practicality that characterized her parenting style. I'll never forget the time I ran to her in tears after Joanna had punched out one of my teeth. Without missing a beat, Mum said, "*do the same back to her.*" The satisfaction of getting permission to punch my sister in the mouth was something I'll never forget. The aftermath was even more memorable—we both ended up crying and laughing, each of us sporting a new gap in our smiles.

On rare occasions, Dad would pick us up, which felt like small celebrations—they always meant ice cream. Despite his demanding schedule, he was the first one up in the morning and the last one to bed at night. We didn't see our parents as much as we would have liked, but they were doing what they had to do to keep everything afloat. I can imagine the judgment from the so-called "*tree-hugging*" parents who might have pointed the finger at mine.

Some of my best childhood memories were made in the playground, playing a game called 'Bundle.' I doubt schools would allow it today, given the strict health and safety regulations. The game was simple yet thrilling—a child would dive to the ground, shouting "Bundle!" and within seconds, a stampede of kids would throw themselves on top, creating a human sandwich of laughter and chaos. To this day, I haven't found anything quite as funny or exhilarating. As a joker who loved attention, I often took the lead, grabbing another boy and shouting "Bundle!" as I pinned him to the ground, both of us dissolving into fits of laughter.

Long Drive was tucked away in a quiet corner of Greenford, but it was alive with the energy of children, including an Asian gang that occasionally crossed our path with flying kicks. Those were the days when you could have a good-natured scrap with someone from a different culture without the heavy shadow of labels like "*racist*" hanging over you. I even sparred with one of these boys years later in a kickboxing class. We both laughed as we recognized each other, realizing that those childhood fights were just a part of growing up, nothing more.

I also recall playing with a grown man when I was about seven. He would pick me up and swing me around above his head, right outside his house. Looking back, I wonder if my parents knew, and if they did, why they never seemed to worry. They understood that I was a bit of a menace, always finding trouble, or they were just too busy.

Sharing bunk beds with my sister was like living in a silent war zone, where the battles were fought in the dead of night. I would lie there, feigning sleep, as I heard her quietly creep out to watch TV from afar. She had this habit of leaning over the balcony at the top of the stairs, and in those moments, a wicked impulse would seize me. I couldn't resist the urge to push her down the stairs. The sound of her crashing into the wardrobe at the bottom was always followed by my muffled sniggers as I quickly buried myself back under the covers, trying to hide the laughter that threatened to give me away. The tell-tale thudding of an unamused parent coming up the stairs usually gave me just enough time to perfect my angelic sleeping pose—Duvet pulled up to my chin, face angelic, butter wouldn't melt in my mouth. Just so long as I did not start laughing when my duvet was pulled down.

Of course, my nocturnal ambushes were just retaliation for her own provocations. She would push her feet onto my top bunk, which inevitably led to me flying off the bed like a ninja. Sometimes she timed it well, catching me asleep.

Dad, in his rare spare moments, would retreat to his sanctuary— his collection of expensive music equipment, a long distant memory from his DJ days. It was his pride and joy, and he made it clear that we were not to touch it in his absence. To keep the peace, we were given a portable tape cassette player, complete with a Disney classics tape. It wasn't long before that innocent Disney tape evolved into Rock 'n' Roll, which I played endlessly, without concern for others. Our quality time with Dad was spent watching *James Bond*, *The Professionals*, and *Spitting Image*, shows that allowed us to bond. Mummy, on the other hand, was usually too busy being mum—her time consumed by the endless demands of running a household.

I still marvel at how Dad, despite his overwhelming schedule, managed to find the time to build an impressive train set in the loft—a miniature world so detailed it could have easily been used by a film studio. Amazingly, Dad said that Mum gave him permission to have a break from the business, and he was always available if need be. But even in this sacred space, there were rules. We were not allowed to touch the controls, and we quickly learned to stay at our designated viewing post, watching in silent awe as the trains circled the tiny, intricate world he had created.

I spent much of the first ten years of my life practically living at the boy next door's house to lose ourselves in endless games of football in their garden or immersing ourselves in the pixelated worlds of *Match of the Day* and *Formula 1* on the ZX Spectrum. Those games, with their painfully slow loading times, taught us a kind of patience that seems almost extinct today. Back then, you had to wait—sometimes a gruelling ten minutes—just to see if the game would load properly. If it crashed, we simply started over, learning resilience in the process. Today's kids have everything at the push of a button, but it was in the waiting, in the anticipation, that we developed maturity and genuinely appreciate the things we wanted so badly.

At school, my main goal was simple: to have fun. I became fast friends with another joker, a kid with a big, infectious smile and a laugh that could light up the room. Together, we turned the classroom into a stage for our antics, bringing joy and laughter wherever we went. Looking back, I sometimes wonder what might have been if I'd had someone to guide me, to mentor me through those chaotic years. But then again, the turbulence of a pubescent mind is a challenge all on its own, one that perhaps no amount of guidance could truly tame.

Home was a playground of its own, especially the stairs, which were a source of endless amusement. Joanna and I would slide down them together on our enormous teddy bear, a furry giant twice our size, hurtling towards the bottom with reckless glee. This was the carefree world of the 70s and 80s, before Health & Safety became the fun police. Sometimes, we'd crash into the wardrobe at the bottom and burst into tears, but if we emerged unscathed, our mum was none the wiser.

Some of my funniest memories involve playing with my next-door neighbour, engaging in the kind of mischief that only kids can devise. We'd hide behind their hedgerow, waiting for cars to drive over our booby trap—a carefully placed blown-up empty drinks carton. The loud pop that followed was our reward, especially if the driver stopped to investigate. We'd dissolve into fits of laughter, the kind that only comes from homemade, free therapy. I still believe there's something deeply therapeutic about indulging in harmless fun, letting your imagination run wild.

Mum had a close friendship with Deryth, a popular childminder who sometimes fed and looked after us kids. Their bond was often sealed with a bottle of wine at our house, where I, true to form, never knew when to stop or keep quiet. My parents, in their frustration, resorted to discipline to try and subdue my boundless energy. After a while, though, I stopped crying when spanked—it was as if even the punishment couldn't dampen my spirit.

At school, diplomacy wasn't exactly my forte, and I often found myself in the deputy headmistress's office. I was a cheeky little so-and-so, a fact that didn't sit well with my dad's short temper. I can only imagine the dreams they must have had, working tirelessly to build a business that we, their children, could one day inherit. The sacrifices they made were immense, but they were sacrifices made with love.

In November 1984, life threw us a curveball. My mum went to visit Deryth in the hospital, who was having her ovaries removed. In a moment of foreboding, mum told her that she should be the one having that operation. As it turned out, she wasn't wrong—Mum had developed a cyst on her ovaries, causing her stomach to swell painfully at night. She was trapped in a prison of her own making, trying to manage the coach business and care for two demanding children. Eventually, she promised Dad that she would have her ovaries out, but only after Christmas.

However, fate showed her cruel side on Boxing Day in 1984. Mum's ovaries, once a source of life, suddenly became a source of destruction as they burst. The doctors discovered they were cancerous, and the disease had already begun its merciless spread throughout her body. Yet, there was a glimmer of hope—Mum received treatment at the Royal Marsden Hospital in London, renowned for its excellence. As a ten year old child, the gravity of the situation was beyond my comprehension. All I knew was that my Mummy was sick, and it tore my heart apart to see her in this fragile, altered state, especially after a stroke left her paralyzed on the left side.

Dad would bring Mum home for day visits, trying to maintain some normalcy in our fractured lives. One day, I was left alone with Mum, just for a moment, but it was long enough to feel an overwhelming surge of pain and confusion. She tried to speak

to me, but the words were lost, trapped somewhere between her mind and her paralyzed body. I couldn't understand her, and my frustration boiled over into tears. I felt so helpless, so lost in that moment, and it must have broken Dad's heart, too, because he never left me alone with Mum again.

We often joined Aunt Sue for walks around Holland Park, but those outings became a source of inner turmoil. Seeing Mum in her wheelchair was a painful reminder of how much had changed, how much we had lost. Sometimes, the emotional weight was too much

to bear, and I would escape to the adventure park, trying to find solace in the simple joy of playing. But even in those moments, there was a gnawing discomfort, a sadness that I couldn't shake. I missed the way we used to laugh together, the way her words used to make sense. Now, they were just sounds, fragmented pieces of a person who was slipping away.

The frustration of not being able to communicate with Mum, of seeing her struggle in her darkest season, was unbearable. I could only imagine the pain and frustration she must have felt, trapped in a body that no longer obeyed her, in a life that had been so cruelly turned upside down.

That summer of 1985, Dad accepted a kind offer from our Godparents, Linda, and Martin, to take my sister and me to Devon. Linda, who had been Mum's best friend since school, opened her home to us, hoping to give us a break from the storm that had engulfed our lives. We spent a few weeks there, trying to find some peace and harmony, surrounded by their two young children. But when they drove us back home, there was a heaviness in the air, a quiet that felt like the calm before the storm.

Dad and Aunt Sue greeted us on arrival. My sister, sensing that something was off, innocently asked why there were flowers everywhere. It was in that moment that Dad, with a voice heavy with grief, told us that Mum had died. The news hit us like a tidal wave, and we both broke down, our small bodies overcome with sobs as we clung to our father. The room, filled with friends and family, became a sea of tears. There wasn't a dry eye in sight.

Aunt Sue, known for her many talents—her fluency in multiple languages, her skill as a classical pianist, and her culinary prowess as a cordon bleu chef—became a beacon of love and compassion during this darkest chapter of my life. It wasn't her expertise that mattered in those moments, but the way she wrapped us in her warmth, her support, and her unwavering care. Her heart, so full of love, became a treasure that I will forever hold dear.

I miss the embrace of my mum and having fun with her. My mummy was someone who wore her heart on her sleeve and never shy or afraid of being silly. I miss her hugs and telling me that she loves me so. I am so proud that people can see streaks of her in me, especially concerning mum's humour. A guardian angel must have sheltered me at the funeral because my behaviour was impeccable, greeting and showing love to everyone.

I thought I just cried my eyes out. A newspaper had pictures of the Royal Hospital Chelsea Pensioners, making a tunnel for the hearse. Going by the numbers in attendance, mum must have made an impression on everyone she knew. How sad that her own mother had also died of cancer.

At the funeral, a pensioner said to dad, *"for Mum's sake, don't sell the business."* This was exactly what Dad had planned to do! However, they did not want to see my dad go, as the Pensioners never had it so good. Everyone said that mum was the brains behind the business, but somehow Dad kept the business going for another decade.

I am so glad for having grown up in the chilled out 70s and 80s, when I was able to seek healing at school via 'Bundle.'

I encourage schools to reintroduce it, as I am proof that it is therapeutic, and that it still makes me smile four decades later.

I grew up as one of two posh kids in Greenford, by virtue of us attending Montpelier Primary School in Ealing. Allegedly, the best in the district. Frustratingly, Jo nor I were able to connect with the other children. Was this because we were outsiders or the fact that we had no idea on how to bond. We played second fiddle to the coach business and were not taught the basics. I hear that the first seven years of a child's life are crucial in character development as an adult, so our guardian angels have been working overtime!

Mum got Deryth to promise to look after us on her deathbed and fate had Deryth and my dad fall in love, despite him having a coach business and two haphazard children and a foul temper.

Deryth's dedication to our family went beyond what anyone could have expected. She not only managed to care for us as a childminder, but she also provided meals and a bed for the coach drivers, supporting Dad in every way she could. Yet, despite her tireless efforts, an unfortunate misunderstanding arose. The drivers saw an advert in the office to sell all the coaches, but Dad had only intended to sell two to reduce the fleet. Fearing the worst, they panicked and left, leaving my father in a difficult position.

Moving in with our stepmother was another chapter of learning and adjustment for my sister and me. We were far from independent, having to be taught even the basics of using public transport. Our new home was one of the nicest in Greenford, a spacious four-bedroom house that stood as a testament to our stepmum's care and organization. Hygiene was paramount under Deryth's watchful eye, and although it felt strict at first, it was exactly what we needed. At the beginning of our time at 195, we might have felt a bit hard done by, struggling to adapt to the new rules and routines.

In my last year at junior school, I noticed a change in the way my peers treated me. For the first time, they started opening their hearts to me, reaching out in ways that were both surprising and comforting. One boy invited me to my first—and, as it turned out, my last—sleepover. The experience ended abruptly when I, struggling to express myself, reacted poorly and punched him in the face. Even the prettiest girl in the history of the school, a vision of kindness and warmth, began to befriend me. She became my first angel, offering solace to my aching heart during a time when I needed it most.

Our first real conversation happened after my mum passed away. She had invited me to her birthday party, where I found myself in heaven, dancing with all the girls and basking in a rare moment of pure joy. For a short time, we would walk to school together, and those walks became the highlight of my days. But as quickly as it began, this beautiful season in my life was cut short, by my own youthful pride or a tinge of jealousy. I may have exaggerated a simple, innocent moment of holding hands, and the delicate connection we had formed was lost.

In those turbulent times, Deryth galloped into our lives like a knight on a trusty steed, bringing with her a silver lining to the cloud that hung over us. She became the steady presence we desperately needed, filling our days with warmth and care. Her culinary skills were legendary in our household, and our taste buds still sing praises of her delicious meals and desserts. Beyond the food, it was the love and patience she showed us that truly made an impression. With her sharp sense of humour and her favourite phrase, "*MYOB* (mind your own business)." Deryth became more than just a stepmother—she became a source of comfort and strength, guiding us through one of the darkest times of our lives with grace and unwavering support.

Why did Mum keep her cancer a secret? Did she long to change her life but found herself trapped, unable to see a way out? Her childhood had been marked by loss and hardship—losing her mother at a young age and living under the care of an unloving stepfather. All while shouldering the responsibility of raising her younger sister, even as an adolescent was forced into a role that shaped her life. My dad, on the other hand, was her opposite in many ways: the only son of a British Army Brigadier growing up with two siblings in a household filled with a different kind of structure and privilege. Their love story began in an unexpected place—a disco in an Ilfracombe hotel, where my dad, the charming DJ, swept my mum off her feet. She was enjoying her newfound freedom with her sister when this handsome coach director appeared, personifying a knight in shining armour coming to her rescue.

After Mum passed away, there were moments of unexpected kindness that brought light into my life. The Chelsea Pensioners, with whom my dad worked, made it possible for me to sit with them in the Director's Box at Chelsea FC. Joining my dad on his job, transporting the Chelsea Pensioners from their barracks to the home matches, and watching matches from the Directors Box until my restless young mind urged me to explore the stadium below.

One game stands out in my memory: Chelsea versus Middlesbrough in the second leg of the play-off final. The Blues needed a 2-0 win to secure promotion back to Division One but only managed a 1-0 victory. What followed the final whistle was a shock—a wave of anger and aggression from some of the home fans that left me transfixed. The sight of a fan attempting to climb over the barbed-wire fence in a frenzy of frustration was unforgettable. I was too young, too fascinated by the chaos around me, to seek safety, but the experience was seared into my memory.

There were lighter moments too, like the time Chelsea played Liverpool, and, despite a 5-2 loss, the atmosphere was electric. Walking with thousands of fans towards the stadium, engulfed in chants and laughter, felt like being part of something grand, something bigger than myself. Their goalkeeper was a real treat to have banter with, especially the time he was at the shed end. Bending over and shaking his rear at us, we chanted "He's bold, he's queer, he takes it up the rear," repeating his name twice, with cries of laughter. Reminiscing always makes me smile!

Amidst all this, I somehow managed to focus on my entrance exam into a military boarding school. I passed and was placed in 1N, the middle class for academic achievement. Looking back, I can't help but wonder what might have been different if we had the chance to redo those years. Time management would have been a priority. Most of all, I think about how a less stressful career might have brought more peace to our family. Yet, despite all the "what ifs," I hold onto the hope that one day I will see Mummy again.

CHAPTER TWO

Boarding School

My grandfather held the last prestigious Army post of Commandant here. From the moment I was born, the path to boarding school seemed inevitable. My dad, having spent his own school holidays there, was sure this was the best place for me. He'd seen it all—the discipline, the grand traditions. He knew it. He believed in it. And, at first, so did I. The idea of a school with its own athletics track that my grandfather designed. For a sports fanatic like me, it sounded like the adventure of a lifetime.

The first time I saw the entrance; I was in awe. The headmaster's house was a sight to behold, just past the security gate. The grounds stretched out in perfect symmetry, immaculate and intimidating. I remember feeling a buzz of excitement during that first meal at the cookhouse—so much food, so many friendly faces. It felt like the world had unfolded in front of me, a promise of something bigger, something prestigious. The dining hall was enormous, like an old railway station, with the walls lined with plaques celebrating past champions. It was overwhelming in its grandeur, like stepping into a history I hadn't yet earned.

And then, there was the RSM (Regimental Sergeant Major)—he recognized my last name. He asked if we were related. The RSM spoke of my grandfather with admiration, telling me how proud he was to have collaborated with him. In those moments, I felt a pressure I couldn't name, a weight on my shoulders to live up to all these expectations, all this history.

Every Saturday night, we'd sit in the day room, polishing our shoes for Sunday's parade inspection, whilst trying to catch snippets of the movie on TV. It was always a balancing act. That Sunday jog around the school perimeter allowed me to shine as I enjoyed running. The boy who often won, the one always caught for smoking, would sprint ahead of us all and he'd often return grinning.

At night, when the lights went out, the dormitory raids began—boys charging into other dorms, shouting "dorm raid," and chaos would erupt. It was fun at first. There was also a game which had the boy climb over all the cubicles…naked! One night, I tried such a feat, and then the unexpected happened. My neighbour accused me of things I didn't even understand, calling me "*gay boy.*" And in that moment, something inside me shifted. I hadn't even known I was doing something wrong, but the way they looked at me—their sneers, their laughter—cut deep. It was like a crack in the foundation, one that would only grow wider as the years went on.

From that moment, I was marked. The nickname stuck, the whispers followed me everywhere, and suddenly, the school I thought was going to be my adventure turned into something far darker.

The teachers were a mixed bag—some inspiring, some indifferent. There was one man, constantly miserable, who would mutter, "*you cretin,*" at anyone who crossed his path. This was wasted on me as I've only recently discovered the meaning. The cruelty was casual, almost expected, but for me, it started to wear down my defences, piece by piece.

My escape came when I was selected for the school ski trip to Switzerland. It was one of the few bright spots in those early years. I felt free on the slopes, and I even made a friend—a beautiful German girl. We wrote letters to each other after the trip, and for a while, I had something good in my life. But then, the bullying worsened. The letters stopped, and I've always wondered if the bullies intercepted them, even replying in my name. They had stolen something precious from me without me ever realizing it.

How times have changed! There were senior citizens, who were somehow invited to befriend boys in the junior house, unsupervised. One took a liking to me, showering me with gifts, inviting me to his London apartment. It was there, in the confines of a cramped elevator, that he pressed himself against me. I'll never forget the way my skin crawled, the shame I felt for not fighting harder. I shoved him away, but the damage was done. I threw his gifts in the bin and tried to forget, but the memories lingered, gnawing at me like a sickness I couldn't shake.

In my first year, I had been a wild spirit, brimming with energy and defiance. But I was quickly humbled when a towering second-year student picked me up and threw me down wrestle mania style with a stretched out knee to catch my back. The impact took my breath away, not just physically but emotionally. I lay there, gasping for air, feeling the weight of my own pride crumble. That moment marked the beginning of a long journey toward self-discovery and restraint. However, the following day, I had recovered and was back with that nonchalant grin!

I then faced a different kind of challenge. When a boy dared to insult my mum, I felt a surge of protectiveness. *"Don't talk about her like that!"* I shouted, my voice trembling with a mix of anger and fear. But the teasing didn't stop. I found myself defending my identity, my worth, against whispers that questioned who I was. Each confrontation was a blow, chipping away at my self-esteem and leaving me raw.

After being summoned to the housemaster's office for the third time, I faced an ultimatum: change or face expulsion. The threat loomed large, and my parents were informed. The conversation that followed was a turning point. My dad's plea for me to change resonated deeply. He spoke of pride, of legacy, especially in the wake of my grandfather's passing. The weight of their expectations bore down on me, a pressure I hadn't fully understood until that moment.

Overnight, something shifted within me. The backbone I once wore with defiance seemed to dissolve, replaced by a yearning to belong and to make my family proud. But the shift didn't go unnoticed; the vultures circled, sensing my vulnerability. I had traded my fighting spirit for conformity, and the battle within me was far from over.

In my second year, I made a mistake that would change everything. In a moment of frustration, I used a racial slur against a boy who had been taunting me. He was mixed-race, popular, and when he retaliated by beating me up, it was in full view of the entire dining hall—including the headmaster. He was suspended, but the damage was done. I became even more of a target.

The dining hall was a place of contrasts, a stage for my best and worst memories. I adored school dinners—their comforting familiarity, the warmth of the food filling the air. But it was here, in the bustling queue, that my innocence collided with cruelty. I made the mistake of questioning a boy who cut in front of me. He was no ordinary boy—he was a bully, with an intimidating presence, even as a child. Before I could grasp the consequences, his hands lifted me off the ground and, with a callous indifference, slammed me headfirst onto the unyielding concrete.

The pain was immediate with an intense searing agony that coursed through my skull and seared itself into my memory. To this day, no physical torment has matched it!

What followed was a quiet torment. I staggered to the medical centre, my vision swimming, my head pounding like a drumbeat of betrayal. The short walk stretched into eternity. I was alone, my footsteps echoing in the hallway. Alone physically, yes, but the real battle raged within. Shame, anger, and confusion clashed in a storm that I could not escape.

When I was home for the school holidays, the neighbourhood football games were my refuge—a brief respite from the pressures and confusion of boarding school life. I wasn't the best player, not by a long shot, but it didn't matter. The boys would often tease me for attending a 'posh' school. I'd shrug it off because I was posh! I just never knew it. One of the non-sporty boys, always lurking on the edges, thought it would be funny to launch an apple at my face with terrifying accuracy while I was perched in a tree. In that split second, more pain, and tears! I felt my blood boil. I scrambled down, fuelled by a surge of anger, chasing him relentlessly through the park until I cornered him by the phone box, near the zebra crossing. No one stopped me. No one cared to. This boy was even more of a public menace! As I pounded my fists into him, I felt something primal and desperate surge from deep within me. The laughter ceased, replaced by uneasy silence. It was never about the apple.

I joined the 2nd XI hockey team, a small but fierce step into a world of camaraderie and competition. When we travelled to Hanau, Germany, it was exhilarating—yet my excitement was shadowed by the teasing that echoed in my ears. My dad, the coach driver, beamed with pride, but that only fuelled the taunts from the boys. "*How could he be your dad?*" they jeered, their laughter ringing out like a cruel symphony. Each comment cut deeper, making me question my identity and connection to the man who meant so much to me.

My eldest stepbrother John and his wife Sue, with their warmth and wit, were the first to make me feel like I truly belonged somewhere. Their kindness was like a lifeline, pulling me back from the edge whenever I felt like I was insignificant. Then there was my stepsister Carol and her jovial, husband Lee who would pop into my life at random intervals, leaving behind warmth and laughter. These fleeting visits, these moments of acceptance, were what kept my heart from fracturing completely. Looking back, I realize they were my emotional glue, holding me together when everything else seemed to be falling apart.

But life, as it does, had its way of complicating things. My parents were always caught up with the endless demands of running a coach company and child-minding, and it felt like there was always another crisis. Even when I desperately needed their attention, something more urgent would arise. I learned early on that my sadness would have to wait. Our family outings to a restaurant were supposed to be a time to connect, but they often dissolved into arguments. We'd go to the cinema afterward, but my parents, worn out from the constant grind, would inevitably fall asleep.

My father, always stressed and short-tempered, spent his days navigating the chaos of work and raising a son who craved his attention. But sometimes, that attention was a sharp slap, its imprint lingering on my skin like a physical reminder of his frustration. I realize now he was struggling too, but back then, all I could feel was the sting of rejection. Oddly, I'm grateful for those moments now because my dad has since developed a sense of humour.

At school, rugby was my sanctuary. I had played mini rugby for Harrow, and I couldn't wait to get back on the field. In junior school, I had patiently played full-back in the B team, always waiting for my moment. And then, in my second year, that moment came—a split-second chance to make the most important tackle of my school career. It was during the annual Junior House match, and this boy, a prodigy of sorts, was streaking towards the corner for what seemed like an inevitable

 try. I hurled myself at him, my body colliding with his, and somehow, against all odds, I stopped him. The housemaster of his junior house even congratulated me afterward, and for the first time in what felt like forever, I felt seen. This was what I had been waiting for—proof that I was capable, that I mattered! It would prepare me for the battles in senior school, though I had no idea the kind of battles I'd face off the pitch.

The teasing became sharper, the looks more scrutinizing. In my senior house, I was starting to be teased by juniors and seniors. Whilst sat in the pool changing room, an older boy from my senior house stood in front of me naked, making me look down in embarrassment. They now knew the truth! The older seniors in the school never did that again. Instead, they just called me 'gay boy,' but in their heart, they knew that I was not. Their words still cut deep, carving out pieces of my identity I wasn't ready to lose.

The bullying was insidious, creeping in like a shadow that darkened every corner of my life. By the fifth form, I had begun to retreat into myself, hiding away in the company of other boys who were also picked on. We were a small, sad cluster of misfits, each dealing with our own private hells. One of them, someone I had considered a friend, came into my cubicle one day, drawing the curtain closed behind him. What followed was confusing—a blur of unwanted advances and misplaced trust. I was overwhelmed by lust, confusion, and guilt. I didn't know how to say no. I didn't even know what was happening to me. The shame wrapped itself around me, tighter and tighter, until I felt suffocated by it. The can of worms was open, and there was no way to close it again.

Despite all of this, I somehow managed to pull myself together long enough to focus on my GCSE exams. It felt like a miracle, as if I were clinging to the last shreds of my sanity by sheer willpower. I got a B grade in Maths and Design. I even built a fiberglass shoe-holder in the shape of a shoe. It was during those long, lonely nights, lying awake in the darkness, that I would turn to the soothing hum of talkback radio. The sound of voices, faceless and distant, became my lullaby, and I found a strange comfort in their chatter. During the day, I buried myself in pop ballads, their melancholic melodies mirroring the sadness I was too scared to express.

How was I going to convince my parents that I absolutely did not want to go back to boarding school for the sixth form? The thought of it made my chest tighten, and I felt a surge of desperation bubbling inside me. I could see no other way forward but to scream hysterically at them—an act that felt both terrifying and a relief, a raw expression of my inner turmoil. It was a moment I dreaded but knew I had to seize, the first and last time I'd let them see just how deeply this affected me.

It didn't matter that my teacher for the proposed BTEC National Diploma was a TA officer—a figure I trusted and respected deeply. In my heart, I knew that no matter how supportive he was, the environment outside of lessons would turn my days into a relentless struggle. I was terrified at the thought of returning to a place that had once felt like a cage.

As I wrestled with my thoughts, uncertainty clouded my mind. What was I going to do? My heart raced as I recalled a conversation with a family member, someone who saw a glimmer of hope in my situation. They had suggested pursuing a BTEC National Diploma in Computer Studies, pointing out that in 1991, this was the future.

The biggest lie that I believed was *"sticks and stones may break my bones, but words will never harm me."* I now know differently.

Words are weapons, and they can leave scars far deeper than any bruise. They cut into your soul, leaving wounds that never fully heal. But through it all, I had Daniel and Toby—the resident Labradors—waiting for me at home. Their unconditional love, their warm, soft fur, and gentle eyes, were the closest thing to therapy I had in those days. Those brief moments with them were my salvation, the rare times when I felt truly safe.

CHAPTER THREE

Transition

At seventeen, I played for a local men's football team, joined by a few mates. The men were much older, much slower—and I didn't mind. It was a laugh, until we faced teams with younger players, and suddenly, the game felt serious. The competition, the stakes, the adrenaline— it was all a rush; especially the one time I scored. It was simple, really: just time the run, attack the near post, and meet the ball with my head. But the moment it hit the back of the net, a feeling surged through me, the kind of pure, unfiltered joy I could barely contain.

Playing football in the park, I saw faces I'd known all my life. I was free from the suffocating walls of boarding school, and in theory, which should have been the moment to find myself, to step out and make new connections. But I tried, and I failed. I wasn't sure what I was looking for, or if I even had the courage to find it. So, I just kept playing, kept running, as if I could outrun the loneliness that gnawed at me beneath the surface.

Like so many young men, I had to learn the hard way, mostly by stumbling through mistakes, by falling, by getting back up and falling again. There was no manual for how to navigate life in those years—just the hope that, one day, I might understand it all.

Then came a mate, a few years older, a familiar face who knew a drugs dealer. At first, I'd just smoked a joint, a freebie passed around, just for the hell of it. But that one spliff slowly became the beginning of something darker. I began using my paper round money to buy more, and with each hit, the numbness I was searching for set deeper into my bones.

It was not long before my smoking buddies took advantage of my lack of a backbone, and survival of the fittest was now in play. I once beat up one of them as a child, who now relished in my passive nature. He persistently called me 'Rodney' or 'Tosser.'

Occasionally, he would also give me a dead arm or leg, as he was now considerably bigger and had the strength to go with it. I was welcome in this gang, as the butt of their jokes, but I did not care. At least now I could numb the pain with lots of laughs, and sometimes I was not even mentioned.

Somewhere in all that mess, I tried to find excitement with adventure. I spent two weeks chasing the ghosts of Spiral Tribe, a treasure hunt for a night that promised freedom, music, and chaos. I kept getting led on, promises of raves that never materialized. But by the third week, something in me snapped. I tracked the rave down to Winchester, took a £60 taxi to get

there. No guarantees, no safety net, yet my prayers were answered. I heard the moderate distant sounds of techno, causing a cheer from the crowd of ravers. This was healing to my soul, whilst walking in the dark with no sense of direction .

When I bumped into my mates there, they were shocked. They must have thought I was mad—but they saw something in me, a raw, desperate yearning to be part of something, anything. They laughed when I told them about the taxi fare, especially as I only had £5 for my travel home. but I didn't care. I'd followed my heart into the unknown, and for once, it felt good.

I remember one evening, when they set me up with a girl, just to see what would happen. No warning, no time to breathe, and certainly no spliff to calm my nerves. I turned red, awkward as hell, fumbling with words that meant nothing. Eventually, one of my them checked up on proceedings, and then I heard laughter in the next room. I can confirm that I never heard from her again.

College was not much better. The BTEC National Diploma in Computer Studies was a struggle—either I relied on teachers throwing me lifelines or endured the ridicule of the class prat, the one who made it his mission to torment me. I walked into college like a lamb to the slaughter—my hand-me-down clothes only making me a bigger target for bullying. I looked different, stood out in all the wrong ways. But I was trying to fit in, trying to be part of something I didn't understand.

The college was made up of 50% Asian and the Blacks and Whites made up the rest. I was made to feel welcome by a friendly Black couple, who introduced me to their friends in the canteen. A week later I managed to get some money together and buy some garments (baggy clothes), so that I would fit in with my peers. And yes, the class prat noticed my change and persisted in abusing me.

I impulsively invited myself to a dance at Greenford town hall, which my canteen mates had talked about. It was at the top of the steep high street and was frequented only by black youths.

Initially, I just stood looking from a safe distance, hoping I would see a familiar face. I did! Popping his head out of the entrance as if looking for me, was a tall friendly man from college. He had a face looking like horror, shaking his head from side to side. I got confirmation of not to go in when three youths walked past me. One of them purposefully barged into my shoulder. Ok Mr Laing, time for you to go home!

I found solace in small things—like playing table tennis, where sometimes I played a member from the slick gang who looked like they owned the world. They were cool, had the girls, and were always laughing. But I had the loudest hidden laugh if I ever beat them, as now they had the shame of being beaten by Rodney. Even if only by sheer luck, it felt like a small victory against everything they'd ever mocked me for. It was the one place I could prove that I wasn't just a joke.

I will never forget the joy I experienced when I twisted up one such adolescent, playing football on route to driving the ball into the bottom corner. Again, my Guardian Angel must have been shining on me as I had two left feet!

It was a miracle that I completed my BTEC, considering that most afternoons I would be stoned after smoking a spliff at lunch with fellow users in the class. Another classmate had an unusual laugh, which sounded like he was choking. He was kind enough to help get me a job at a supermarket in Ealing, where he & other students from the college also worked.

It was here that my heart was reignited by the prettiest girl from my class at primary school. All she had to say was *"hello Alex."* She was a with a model type male, and that was the last I saw of her. I used to help myself to sweets, which were loose. One day my manager caught me eating, whilst working. He asked me if I had taken the sweet from the loose packet, and I impulsively spoke the truth. Time for a change!

At college I become friendly with a girl, who once gave me a kiss on the lips. All I could do was turn red, displaying my embarrassment! She never bothered me again. The icing on the cake of my college experience was the teacher overseeing an exam saying, *"don't do anything I wouldn't do,"* as he walked outside for approximately ten minutes.

I had a fervent desire for a quieter life, so I left home. Dad was kind enough to drive me to the council office, where I sat for the remainder of the day with my belongings in plastic carrier bags. This was back in the day when you could just turn up at the council and be housed on the same day. They called my parents to confirm my status before I faced the Krypton Factor of taking a bus.

My home was a B&B in Southall aka little India and l was now in a stress free environment where l could listen to my hardcore music, whilst smoking dope. I was the only white person in the B&B. I was made to feel welcome, but a bit too much by one housemate. He bought back a woman from the pub and after being intimate with her, he asked me if I fancied a go. I politely declined.

Months later, I fare dodged the train every two weeks, the rumbling tracks a constant reminder of how far I'd fallen. From Luton to Southall, just to pick up my benefit cheque—my only source of income.

"*Hello Groundhog Day*" where nothing seemed to change. I'd enrolled in the next course, thinking I could redeem myself after the disaster I'd made of the last one. What a plonker I was! I had picked Luton as my home, not for its promise, but because it was where the girl I'd fancied from college was living. But instead of studying, I was just pretending. Doing nothing. I'd become so good at it, that when I asked a tutor for help, he just pointed me to the library. A cold slap in the face after college, where tutors would've gladly spoon-fed me if I'd asked. Reality hit hard. It was as if I'd been caught naked in a world that didn't care about excuses.

I started selling weed at the university. For the first few weeks, I convinced myself I was living the high life—status, attention, respect. The kind of respect that lasts about as long as it takes to roll a joint. It wasn't until I met my housemate's friend, a slick, gangster type, that I realized how naive I really was. Wanting to impress this girl, I boasted about my "*business*." Big mistake. The next day, this guy—smooth as hell—talked me into handing over my stash, telling me he'd help me sell it. A gut-wrenching realization. I had nothing. Not even control over my own life.

I made friends with a group of girls, who I spent much time with, including meals and a smoke after. I even got to share one of their bed's and even made a move. She turned away my advances, so I stopped. A week later, she had a new boyfriend, who had a better understanding in the art of persistence.

Most weekends, I lost myself in the thumping beats of the drum & bass bars on Luton High Street. The haze of smoke, the flashing lights—it was like I was floating through life with no anchor. No purpose. And yet, somehow, I didn't care. Until the day I showed a shred of common sense—finally. I quit. I left that world behind. At least for a while.

Then came the night I took LSD at a Spiral Tribe in Uxbridge. A naive first-timer, I took some, impatiently waiting for it to hit. I took another one an hour later. By the time I was back at my B&B, it was too late. The acid took hold, and I found myself trapped in the music, the sharp clarity of it almost paralyzing me. I freaked out when someone asked me for food. I couldn't even make a sandwich. I freaked out! It was my first and last time touching LSD, but it sure left its mark.

Drugs kept calling, and soon enough, I tried Ecstasy. At a mate's house party, I took a tablet and let the flood of euphoria wash over me. At first, it felt like I could conquer the world. I felt like a stud in season as I tried talking to a woman, but my words came out in a slurred mess. Pathetic! That's how I felt, even as I rushed to the kitchen to drink some water to cool off the heat that was building up inside me. But nothing helped. In a panic, I stumbled out the front door for some fresh air—but I collapsed. My face scraped against the brick as I fell. When I looked up, I saw my mate smiling at me. Great!

I nearly got run over, whilst stoned up. The driver recognized me, by virtue of being friends with Deryth. I was duly invited home, in order that I sort my life out. My dad's work colleague, an ex-Guards officer, must have mentioned that the Air Corps was the future of the British Army. On my arrival back home I was told that I needed to sort my life out! That I was going to join the Army Air Corps and that was that!

At the outbreak of WW1, my Great-Grandfather transferred from the Gordon Highlanders to the Royal Flying Corps. He joined as a CSM (Company Seargent Major) and ended the war as a half Colonel! On the RAF becoming established, he transferred, losing a rank to Squadron Leader. He retired as Air Vice Marshall, Sir George Laing. My Grand-Father retired as a Brigadier in the Duke of Wellington's, where he also displayed his sports prowess in rugby and cricket.

My dad earned his commission in the Territorial Army section of the Royal Corps of Transport and retire as a Captain. He displayed determination and commitment, as he had already been medically discharged from the Army Catering Corps. He must have hoped that I would keep the family tradition of becoming an officer as a pilot.

My mates—my so-called friends—couldn't understand it. They were anti-establishment, anti-everything. They thought I'd fail. But I didn't care. I was ready to leave behind the mess I'd created, ready to move forward, even if I had no idea what the future held.

I went to Amsterdam with a naive, last-ditch attempt at proving I was still in control. I came back ashamed, having been fleeced and humiliated, but that trip marked the end of one chapter. It was time for something new.

Back home, I continued smoking with my mates until one eventful evening. I was dropped home after midnight, but he reversed up the drive to set the lights off and beep his horn. That evening, I received so much verbal abuse.

I was now livid and wanted revenge. The next day he answered his door all smiles. We started arguing and so took it outside. I surprised myself and this man as I released all my suppressed aggression, which had been built up since childhood. He was out boxed, and in response he told me to wait whilst he got his knife.

I did not hang about and started to run away! Whilst walking home I was pulled over by the police as my top was ripped and covered in blood. After explaining what had happened, they went to his address with me in the back to validate my story. Later in the day, the man in question turned up at my door to vent his anger for calling the police on him. He also had to get stitches for his nose. His leaving comments were *"If I ever see you again, I'm going to stab you!"* Proof, that you cannot please everyone.

I was now ready to join the Army.

My parents were quietly pleased with my outcome but were gracious enough not to rub it in. I was done with my past. Done with the person who had let people walk all over him, done with the person who could barely look himself in the mirror. I was ready to be someone different.

I started preparing physically, running laps around the athletics track in Perivale, focusing on the future. I pushed myself harder than I ever had before. I alternated between 3 x 400m sprints and 3 x 1500m runs, sometimes throwing in shuttle sprints for good measure. My legs ached, my lungs burned, but I welcomed the pain. It felt good. It felt real. I was finally taking control of something.

The entrance exams at the Army Careers Office were gruelling, but I passed in the top half. I could now choose between the (AAC) Army Air Corps and the (RMP) Royal Military Police. Temptation was in the midst to join the RMP as I also had a brief time as a volunteer police cadet prior to leaving home.

I walked out of there with a sense of pride that had been foreign to me for so long. I wasn't the screw-up anymore. I wasn't the laughing- stock. I was a man on a mission, with a sense of purpose.

Prior to Basic Training, I had to complete a 24-hour selection at the Army Training Centre in Pirbright, Woking. The selection included a mile-and-a-half run and other exercises completed early in the morning.

It wasn't about escaping anymore. It was about becoming someone I could respect. Someone I could look in the mirror and be proud of. It wasn't about living up to anyone's expectations, but my own.

That's when I knew it was time to leave the past behind, for good.

I had survived. Survived the drugs, the fights, the mistakes, the loneliness. There were moments—too many moments—when I thought I wouldn't make it. But I had.

When I look back on those days, the ones when I stumbled through life with no real direction, I see how far I've come. I'm not proud of everything I did, but I wouldn't change it. It shaped me, moulded me into someone different. Someone stronger. Someone who was finally ready to take the next step, even if it meant walking away from everything I knew.

It wasn't the life I had imagined when I was younger, but that's the point. Sometimes, the hardest battles are the ones we fight with ourselves—learning who we are, and, more importantly, who we want to be.

In the end, my guardian angel must have been watching over me—because I'd survived every single mess I'd created, every bad decision, and now, at last, I was ready for something bigger than myself.

CHAPTER FOUR

Army Air Corps

People join the Army for different reasons: some dream of adventure and the chance to see the world, others crave the rush of action. And then there are those like me, who needed something more—structure, discipline, a sense of purpose. As my dad put it, I needed "a kick up the backside!"

I was supposed to begin Basic Training in April 1996, but a football injury—a dislocated right thumb—forced me to delay my start. Instead of joining in the spring, I was pushed back to the July intake. The first hurdle was the 24-hour selection at Pirbright Barracks, followed by a trip to the Army Careers HQ in London. There, I was asked to swear allegiance to the Queen. It was a surreal moment.

The Colonel glanced at my details and remarked, with a hint of surprise, how I had survived a stint at that boarding school. "Well done, old boy," he chuckled, clearly impressed. That simple comment felt like a weightlifting off my shoulders. It was the first time someone acknowledged my battle with bullying, and it filled me with an unexpected sense of accomplishment.

Before I set off for Basic Training, my dad gave me one last piece of advice, "Just imagine it'll be like living your worst nightmare." It was blunt, but it worked. When I finally arrived, I was ready. And to my surprise, after only a few days, I started to thrive.

Basic Training

When I stepped onto the grounds of Winchester, the reality of Army life hit me. We were split into sections within our platoon, and each group was introduced to their Cpl (Corporal), a man of few words. In fact, he hardly spoke at all. If he had something to say, it came in the form of a scream or a shout, usually directed at someone—usually us. In my section, four of us were often the target of his vocal fury. And, yes, I was one of them.

Admin was my Achilles' heel. The constant pressure of being yelled at made it hard to keep track of orders and instructions.

There were times when my mind went blank, and I found myself scrambling to catch up, acting like a headless chicken. I couldn't help it. When the commands came fast and sharp, they were hard to process, let alone remember. But each time I stumbled, I found a little more resolve.

Even in those moments of confusion and frustration, something inside me clicked. The rhythm of Army life—the discipline, the focus, the constant push to be better—began to settle into my bones. Little by little, I was finding my footing, and with each passing day, I was becoming more than just a recruit; I was becoming part of something bigger. The nightmare was slowly turning into a dream I didn't want to wake up from.

As punishment, I was often tasked with long-distance runs, combined with gruelling sets of press-ups. The runs were brutal, but I had a bit of an edge—I was consistently one of the top runners, coming third in the mile and a half. My Cpl saw this as a strength and quickly figured out how far he could push me. The reality of Basic Training was simple: it was about breaking us down so we could be rebuilt into disciplined soldiers.

The recruits in our platoon ranged in age from 17 to 25, and I was right in the middle at 21. A quarter of us were women, and their presence added a dynamic to the platoon that I hadn't anticipated.

The humour was dark, sometimes cruel. One recruit, was notorious for sweating—so much so that every day he was mocked relentlessly *"You sweat like a paedophile in a playground!"* The Cpl would scream as he pushed his mattress and bedding out of the window.

We would help each other get our rooms in perfect order before inspections, but this one recruit would always fidget with his layout at the last minute, moments before our Cpl arrived to inspect. At some point, we just gave up trying to help him. We'd let him do his thing and brace ourselves for the inevitable storm that followed.

There were four sections in our platoon, each under the command of its own Cpl, and our Sgt (Sergeant) would usually lead the parades. The OC (Officer in Charge) was the one who taught us the history and subjects related to the AAC, and I'll never forget the Sgt's simple yet powerful words: "If you think something is rubbish, you have to say why."

Exercise Halfway

It was during Exercise Halfway that everything seemed to click. This wasn't just another test—it was the ultimate test of our teamwork, our fitness, and the skills we had learned so far. The exercise felt like the shift we had all been waiting for. There was something about it that gave us a renewed sense of purpose. But as any seasoned soldier knows, presumption is the mother of all errors. Confidence was important, but overconfidence can leave us exposed. And as we soon found out, as this exercise was meant to push us to our limits—and beyond. It was a wake-up call, showing us what we were truly made of. We had to rely on each other more than ever before. In that moment, we learned that strength wasn't just physical ability, but about being part of a team that never gave up, no matter how tough things got.

It was a sweltering day, the sun beating down relentlessly. We were all in the prone position in our newly built dugouts, filled with a mix of anticipation and anxiety. The dugouts were strategically placed in a triangular formation, giving us a solid defensive position with coverage from all sides. But despite the perfect setup, there was one glaring issue that gnawed at all of us: the jerry cans of water were placed just within sight of the DS (Directing Staff), and we were forbidden from drinking any of it. The water was tantalizingly close, yet completely out of reach.

For me, this was breaking point. I could feel my body growing desperate for hydration. My throat felt like sandpaper, and I couldn't suppress the urge to drink any longer. Before I could even swallow a gulp, I was reprimanded. The DS, always watching, never missed a beat. Without warning, I was handed a pickaxe and ordered to start hauling myself around the perimeter of our harbour, moving at a pace that made my legs scream in protest. I couldn't argue—I had no choice but to comply, sweating even more as I circled the perimeter, the heat and fatigue starting to feel unbearable.

But if there was one thing I'd mastered by this point, it was enduring discomfort, and it wasn't long before my embarrassment faded into a sort of grim determination.

I also made history by being the first recruit to lose my firing pin whilst on exercise Halfway! My Cpl had to ensure that I understood that I had made a serious mistake. I then felt obliged to carry my rifle above my head whilst running to another landmark on the horizon.

We were also shown how to use our rifle as a machine gun. Whilst cleaning my rifle, I made the mistake of not switching the shooting mode back to single shot. I only realised this was so once the sound of continuous fire was omitted. I was screamed at to make my weapon safe and then, as expected, came the punishment. They kicked the stuffing out of me. It was a mixture of tough love and harsh correction, but in that moment, I couldn't help but think how absurd the whole thing was. The situation, though tense, struck me as strangely hilarious. I played along, instinctively covering my head and ribs, pretending to be in pain to avoid further wrath.

I knew the drill by now—show weakness, and the DS would pounce. But if you could find a way to laugh in the face of the madness, to find humour even in the harshest moments, you could survive.

In those moments, I realized something about myself: that it wasn't the mistakes that defined me, but how I responded to them. If I could take the beating, both physical and mental, and still get back up each time, then I was building something stronger inside me—something the Army couldn't break.

As I stood tall and slim, I knew my upper body lacked the strength it needed. I felt the weight of my own shortcomings, a mix of frustration and determination surging through me as I practiced chin-ups on the branch of an old tree. That branch became my silent adversary, a symbol of the resilience I was trying to build. The looming BFT (Basic Fitness Test) wasn't just a requirement; it was a test of my will. Comp- leting a one-and-a-half mile run in under ten minutes thirty seconds was a breeze, and the sit-ups felt like clockwork. But those six bar-heaves? They were my Everest.

I'll never forget the sting of struggling with five heaves, my muscles burning, and my breath shallow as I pushed for the sixth. The PTI, sharp-eyed and ever watchful, counted in their maddeningly precise way. "Five," they called, their tone a mix of dismissal and challenge. I knew in my heart I had done six. I felt it in the ache of my arms and the strain in my soul. Yet they let a few of us sweat it out for twenty agonizing minutes, leaving us to question ourselves before they revealed the truth. That sly grin on their faces wasn't just mockery—it was a lesson in patience, grit, and the importance of holding your own under pressure.

It wasn't until the passing out parade celebrations that I discovered the camp's bar. Up until then, I'd been too consumed by the gruelling demands of training to notice much else. Some of the men had made a ritual of slipping into the NAAFI for a few pints, often returning just in time for reveille, their stories layered with bravado and fleeting entanglements. I, however, didn't have that luxury—or, truthfully, the energy. Basic Training had wrung me dry, leaving little room for anything but sheer focus and effort.

When we finally gathered at the NAAFI for a quick drink, it felt like stepping into a world I barely recognized. From there, we waited for our chariots to take us into Winchester. That night was a revelation. For the first time in ages, I felt a surge of confidence as I spoke to a woman in town. She had a lisp, but her warmth and openness made it irrelevant. It was a small, ordinary moment, but to me, it was extraordinary—a glimpse of the person I was becoming. The next day, I learned of the rumours swirling about me, the cheeky suggestion that I had sex with a girl in a wheelchair.

It was classic Army humour—crass, absurd, and strangely endearing. Welcome to the brother-hood, Air Trooper Laing.

The following day was a whirlwind of finishing touches to our kit and preparing to meet our guests. I felt a profound sense of pride as I stood tall in my uniform, reflecting on how far I had come. The inspecting officer's words were like a seal of approval on my transformation. He had played a pivotal role in the success of the Falklands War, and his encouragement felt like a torch being passed.

When my parents and sister arrived, their pride was visible. For the first time in years, I felt their affirmations pierce through the walls I had built around myself. This moment, this milestone, was more than just the culmination of Basic Training—it was a victory over the shadows of my past. The boy who had carried the weight of a traumatic childhood had grown into a man standing on the threshold of a new life. I wasn't bitter anymore. Instead, I felt the quiet satisfaction of closure and facing my demons.

Driving School Training (DST), Leconfield – near Hull

For Ground Crewmen in the AAC, an HGV license is essential—a gateway to operating fuel bowsers, 4-ton trucks, and land rovers. The next chapter of my training took me to DST Leconfield in Yorkshire, a sprawling facility that instantly dwarfed any expectations I had. It was our first rendezvous since passing Basic Training, and while I was excited to move forward, I carried a lingering uncertainty—especially when it came to interacting with women. My confidence was still a work in progress.

Sharing the dormitory with soldiers from different corners of the Army brought its own quirks. One evening, I was unoccupied. "*Try this,*" he said with a mischievous grin and within seconds, my world spun. I had to lie down from the dizzying rush, where I was reminded of my raving days and the music sounded clearer than ever. I couldn't stop grinning. Flippin heck, Laing! I thought, laughing at myself. Years later, I learnt that '*poppers*' were popular within the gay community for loosening up the rectum—an awkward discovery that left me both bewildered and amused. I still remember that soldier with his black beret and persistent smile.

Leconfield had its moments, but it wasn't without its challenges. The sprawling campus could feel isolating, and the loneliness hit hardest on weekends. During those times, I often found solace in the NAAFI bar, nursing a cup of tea, and chatting with a kind member of staff. Looking back, I would strongly encourage anyone training at DST to lean on the welfare services—those quiet moments of connection can make a world of difference.

The experience reminded me of my boarding school days: the same stretches of monotony, the same bouts of depression and boredom. Still, I showed persistence and grit to complete my HGV training, even when it meant repeating tests. Passing felt like a hard-won victory, a testament to my determination to keep moving forward despite the hurdles.

Middle Wallop

In early 1997, I was enlisted on a Class B3 Ground Crewman course, my next step in becoming part of the AAC. Arriving at Middle Wallop, I stepped out of the taxi and into the guardroom with a mixture of anticipation and trepidation. For the first few hours, I felt as though I had a target on my back, constantly glancing over my shoulder. The paranoia of a corporal lying in wait to catch me off guard kept me on edge, but thankfully, nothing materialized.

The transition was surreal. It felt like stepping into a new chapter, one filled with challenges and opportunities I hadn't yet fully grasped. The reception I received at 2 Trg Regt (Training Regiment) AAC would set the tone for my journey ahead, but in those early moments, I was focused on finding my footing and squaring everything away.

What a refreshing change from Basic Training—more civilized yet still rooted in the discipline and camaraderie of military life. Middle Wallop, the Headquarters of the AAC, felt like a world apart. Here, soldiers were treated with respect, but only up to a point. If we got too familiar, reality would hit like a sledgehammer, often in the form of a sergeant's bellowing voice.

Despite the occasional shouting, the staff at 668 Trg Sqn were excellent at their jobs, balancing discipline with effective training. The OC even picked me to represent the squadron in obstacle races, recognizing my knack for endurance events. Those races pushed me to my limits, but they also made me proud to carry the banner of my unit.

One of the unexpected thrills of ground crewman training came with the mighty Chinook helicopters. Walking away from one as it powered up was an experience unlike any other. The downwash from the blades was so intense that it could momentarily lift me off the ground, especially when extra torque was applied to haul a 4-ton Bedford truck into the air. It was exhilarating, a reminder of the sheer power of the machines we worked with.

Much of our training revolved around the Lynx MK7 aircraft, often out on Salisbury Plain. Refuelling and re-arming these helicopters in the field was as demanding as it was rewarding. There was something undeniably cool about being ferried to strategic points on the plain in a Lynx—a front-row seat to the action, and a chance to feel like a key part of the mission.

Not all moments went smoothly, of course. One memorable day, I was tasked to drive down Andover High Street. Approaching the rendezvous, I misjudged the turn and ended up ditching the vehicle. My navigator, unexpectedly, was launched onto the pavement, where his cheek made an unceremonious landing. A nearby police officer arrived within moments, asking him if he wanted to press charges for assault. His face now sported a war wound—a testament to our misadventure—but instead of anger, we burst out laughing. "You're sound," he assured the WPC, brushing off the mishap as we both retrieved our trolley of a vehicle. It was one of those moments that cemented the bond between us, a shared story we'd carry with us.

To commemorate my journey to becoming an Air Trooper, I got my first tattoo alongside some of the other recruits. I chose a tiger's head on my back shoulder—a nod to my childhood nickname, *Tiger*, earned during my mini rugby days. The tattoo was more than just ink; it was a badge of pride, marking how far I'd come.

The culmination of our training brought a posting of twenty-one soldiers to 1 Regt AAC in April 1997. The anticipation in the air was electric as we prepared for life overseas. It was the beginning of a new chapter, one filled with adventure, challenges, and the camaraderie that had become the backbone of our shared experience.

1 Regt AAC - Princess Royal Barracks, Gutersloh, Germany

Once a bustling RAF base, PRB (Princess Royal Barracks) was in the suburbs of Gutersloh, North Germany, and managed by a skeleton staff. Sharing the base with three regiments from the RLC (Royal Logistics Corps), 1 Regt AAC brought its own distinctive energy to the barracks. PRB was a place where tradition and modern Army life blended seamlessly—a hub for discipline, mischief, and the occasional sunlit escape.

My time with MT (Motor Transport) 651 Sqn (Squadron) was, without a doubt, the most fun I've ever had. The credit for that goes to my sergeant and comrades, a troop brimming with some of the best characters in the Regiment, even the Corps. The sergeant himself was a Jekyll & Hyde figure who kept us on edge with his questionable smile and raised eyebrows. At first, his cheery facade lulled many of us into a false sense of security, but experience quickly taught me to stay on my guard. Those telltale expressions were the precursor to whatever mischief he had planned. For the troop, it usually meant raucous laughter at someone else's expense.

The kind, intelligent, and hilariously witty sergeant from Signals Troop left a lasting impression on me. He was my first point of contact when I arrived at the Regiment, and his warm welcome made all the difference. Admin wasn't my forte, but he had the patience of a saint and the humour of a stand-up comedian, which made even the dullest tasks bearable.

HQ Squadron was my final posting with 1 Regt AAC, and it lived up to its reputation. The squadron attracted the Regiment's elite signals personnel, and it was an honour to work alongside such a resolute and professional group. Among them was a standout figure—a sensual soldier who managed the stores with unparalleled commitment. His work ethic and charisma left a lasting impression, embodying the best of what the Regiment stood for.

PRB wasn't all about work, though. It had its fair share of legends, none more iconic than the *Spice Boys*. Handsome and fully aware of it, they were the living embodiment of the Air Corps' unofficial motto: *"Make love, not war."* As members of the 1 Regt AAC football team, they were as skilled on the pitch as they were at charming the barracks. Any hint of sunshine was an excuse for them to fire up a BBQ. With a football at their feet, a beer in hand, and Indie music blasting in the background, they transformed the barracks into a lively, carefree retreat. They were the heartbeat of PRB's social life, and their infectious energy reminded everyone to enjoy the moment, no matter how intense the workday had been.

In Germany, life felt different—lighter, freer, and oddly rewarding. Everything was cheaper than back home in the UK, and as if that weren't enough, we even got an extra £150 per month just for the privilege of being stationed there. It was a peculiar sense of indulgence, both financial and social. Opportunities for adventure abounded, but too often we squandered them in a haze of alcohol, seeking release from something we couldn't quite name.

The Spice Boys, all worked in HQ Squadron, save for one—a striking exception who belonged to 652 Squadron. He fit the mould in his looks, but the rest of him…well, let's just say it was impossible not to notice. How could you not, when they'd strip down to play naked football on the grass in front of our accommodation block? The sheer audacity of it all was baffling yet oddly endearing. I'd often think, *"what am I doing looking?"* But those wild games were hard to ignore.

HQ Squadron had its quirks—our barracks were surprisingly spacious, flanked by a broad stretch of grass that became a playground for these antics. The fun, the frolics—it all seemed surreal. I sometimes wondered if my dad had ever lived through anything like this during his Army days. Somehow, I doubted it. Then again, he was a handsome chap too. My dad could have been one of the *Beach Boys*. The thought amused me.

Amid the chaos of Germany, my mind often drifted back to my basic training days. One memory burned bright. There was a rugby player from my section, larger than life, brimming with confidence. He dove headfirst into playing as soon as we arrived at PRB Gutersloh in July 1997. Meanwhile, I was still adjusting, grappling with the shift and the scrutiny that came with my lean frame. Weak—that's what they saw when they looked at me.

This guy made it his mission to remind me I'd never make it as a flanker because someone else already held the position. His words didn't defeat me. Instead, they ignited something fierce in my core. My stature may have been unimpressive, but my aggression made up for it. I tackled hard, often paying the price with concussions, but I didn't care. Every hit, every struggle was proof that I belonged—that no one could write me off.

Life on camp was nothing if not eventful. Among its offerings was a bar and a disco called *The Bop*, the epicentre of nightly chaos where most soldiers inevitably found themselves. I'm proud to say I only had one run-in with the RLC there, though it was a memorable one. Fuelled by a few too many drinks, my humour didn't land well with one man, and he landed a black eye on me in return. The sting sobered me up instantly.

Something switched inside me—a cold, calculated focus. I kept my eyes on him, manoeuvring through the crowd to the side like a predator stalking its prey. My target was the edge of the dancefloor! I poured my pint over his head to guarantee his attention the moment he turned, I launched myself at him with a flying head-butt, driving him to the ground. Before anyone could react, I followed up with a few quick punches, relishing the rush before security dragged me off. My victory was short-lived—outside, three of his mates were ready for round two. It didn't take long to realize I was out- numbered. Cue: *"run, Forrest, run!"*

Not all escapades were as chaotic. Sometimes we'd head into the town centre, riding the train just to sit outside a café and watch the world go by. More specifically, watching women walk by aka 'letching'—a pastime that required no small amount of beer and banter. Once, we stumbled into a sex shop on the high street, curious about what German liberalism had to offer. To our amazement, there were private cubicles with comfy chairs,

TVs, side tables, kitchen roll, and bins. Proof that the Germans are an accommodating bunch.

But Germany wasn't all mischief and madness. Within three weeks of arriving at PRB, I hit the jackpot: an adventurous training course at Paderborn Aerodrome. Parachuting had always been a dream of mine, and now the Army were footing the bill. Progress was slow for me; where a paratrooper officer breezed through to 1 minute freefall jumps, where I struggled to move beyond the static line.

I'll never forget the first time the plane door opened at 3,500 feet. The rush of air, the deafening roar, and that gut-wrenching mix of terror and exhilaration hit me all at once. The women were always first to jump—whether by tradition or psychology, I'll never know—but I felt sympathy for them. Watching someone else go first didn't make the leap any easier.

The evenings after training were a balm for the nerves. I'd often unwind with another soldier from 1 Regt AAC, swapping stories and sharing laughs. Those moments of camaraderie were the threads that held everything together in the whirlwind of life on base. Germany was a rollercoaster of thrills, mistakes, and milestones, each memory etched deeper than the last.

The streets of Paderborn were immaculate, not a scrap of litter in sight, a testament to the city's orderliness. It was almost ironic, then, that I found myself disrupting this perfection in the most primal way possible. As we walked back to camp, I felt an urgent churn in my gut. My bowels were in full rebellion, and I had no time to spare. Between two parked cars and the curb, I dropped my pants and let nature take its course. The relief was euphoric—an oddly satisfying rebellion against the pristine backdrop of Paderborn's streets. If the police, so meticulous in keeping order, had seen me, I might not have been so triumphant.

Life in Germany was a whirlwind of antics and newfound confidence. My tendency to speak before thinking quickly earned me a reputation as a joker. For the first time in my life, I wasn't just surviving—I was *living*, embracing every moment even when others laughed at my expense. This was my season of fun, and I wasn't about to let it slip away.

Fate has a sense of humour, reuniting me with three elder boys from the same senior house at school, all stationed at PRB. One of them, now a civilian guard, caught me off guard with a comment I'll never forget: *"Alex, you're the last person I expected to see join the Army."* I couldn't help but grin. His words were a reminder of just how far I'd come. The bullying, the doubts, the weight of being underestimated—it all seemed so distant now. Another layer of my past was lifted, leaving me freer than ever.

The camaraderie in Germany had its quirks, to say the least. Drunken newcomers—nigs (new in Germany) as they were labelled—often woke up to cigarette ash smeared across their faces, courtesy of their more seasoned peers. And if the Corps deviant was around? God help them! His favourite party trick involved using their finger as a paintbrush to smear his own pooh on their face. A disturbing initiation, but one that became an infamous tale told over countless beers.

Among my closest mates were three men I'd grown tight with—two from Basic Training and another from the previous intake of soldiers. We were a pack bound by a shared love of dancing, drinking, and endless laughter. Our first major adventure together was the stuff of legends. Of all the places we could've chosen for our first 'Jolly Boys Outing' we went straight for the heart of liberalism: Amsterdam.

Jolly Boys Outing

The city called to us with its promise of freedom and chaos, and we answered eagerly. It was a perfect playground for four young soldiers chasing thrills and stories to last a lifetime.

That night in Amsterdam was one for the ages—a chaotic blend of hilarity, mischief, and hazy memories that we'd laugh about for years to come. Things didn't start smoothly. No matter where we went, we couldn't get into any nightclubs. Our British accents immediately flagged us as troublemakers, thanks to the reputation left by our predecessors who were more fists than fun. After being turned away for the umpteenth time, we gave up and wandered into the next bar we could find.

The atmosphere wasn't what we had planned, but it didn't matter. Three of us decided a bottle of tequila was the solution to our frustrations, while the fourth opted for Pernod and lemonade. The drinks flowed, our laughter grew louder, and we acted daft in the way only drunk young men can. We might have been daft, but we weren't fighters—not that the locals cared to know the difference.

Those friends were exactly what I needed at the time. Their endless humour and camaraderie helped patch up my broken heart, each laugh soothing wounds I hadn't even realized were still raw. Eventually, though, we pushed the limits of our welcome. The bartender refused to serve us more alcohol. Taking the hint, we stepped outside and were greeted by the biting cold of the Amsterdam night.

That's when things went from amusing to absurd. A lorry rumbled past, and my inner joker couldn't resist. I leaped onto its side, clinging to the metal like a stuntman. The driver slammed the brakes and pulled over, storming out of the cab with a face like thunder. He was enormous, shouting something in his local dialect that I couldn't understand but could feel. We burst into laughter, tears streaming down our faces, which only infuriated him further. He shook his fist, bellowing more obscenities before eventually giving up and driving off in frustration. It was a moment straight out of a comedy sketch.

Things grew hazier after that. Mr Pernod and I stuck together while the other two vanished into the night. At some point, he went into a grocery store. When he came out, I was nowhere to be found. But as he scanned the street, he noticed people walking around an obstruction. Upon closer inspection, it was *me*—sprawled out on the ground like a human traffic cone. He called my name, shook me awake, and managed to get me to my feet.

The next thing I knew, I vomited myself awake, whilst sat on a toilet. Groggy and confused, I stumbled into the bedroom, only to realize something wasn't right. The room I found myself in didn't have four single beds like ours. Instead, there was a double bed—and a couple sleeping soundly in it.

I stood frozen, piecing together the night's fragmented events. How I ended up in *their* room, I'll never know. One thing was certain: this was a story for the books, a night where the line between chaos and comedy blurred, leaving us with memories we'd recount endlessly, each time laughing a little harder than the last time.

I don't know what came over me—just pure confusion and panic. I needed to get out, to escape from the chaos of that night. I rushed upstairs to our room, hoping to find my comrades. I did! Asleep outside the door, wrapped in their own exhaustion. A wave of frustration and relief hit me all at once. I checked my pocket, my stomach sinking when I realized the room key was gone. I had to wake them. I had to explain. With a jolt, I shook them awake, a desperate edge to my voice. "*I've lost the room key,*" I blurted out, as if saying it aloud would make it less real.

Without a word, one of my mates groggily sat up, rubbed his eyes, and, with a sheepish smile, held up the key. Somehow, amid the confusion and haze, he had completely forgotten he was the one holding it.

One of them shared his tale of being robbed and beaten up—his voice laced with that strange mix of disbelief and humour. But it was his partner who truly lightened the mood. He gleefully told the story of how he found himself in a train station surrounded by junkies. His only means of survival. Pretending to be insane and doing it convincingly. The absurdity of it all made me laugh, but in that laughter, I could feel the weight of everything we had just endured.

Then someone asked me for the time. I felt for my wrist where my watch should've been—and it wasn't there. It was a punch in the gut. I replied, *"I don't have my watch,"* trying to shrug it off, but my voice cracked with the realization. *"Check your wallet, Al,"* he said, casually. My heart sank as I pulled an empty pocket. *"Damn it!"* Then, amidst my own disbelief, the whole room burst into laughter again. And, for some strange reason, it was comforting. In that moment, the tragedy of it all was shared. It wasn't just my loss—it was all of ours. And somehow, that made it a little bit easier to bear.

Years later, I would remember that night—though not for the chaos or the loss. I remembered how I had been saved by something as simple as a lamp post. After being pulled to my feet by Mr. Pernod—my trusty companion—I felt like I was floating through the night, each step uncertain, as we stumbled along the canal. The world seemed blurry, but the danger was clear. As we wandered, we encountered local opportunists, eyes gleaming with intent. I had been reckless, too generous for my own good. But my comrade, he had his wits about him—he kept his wallet.

And then, the police arrived, pulling us into their world. They began questioning my friend, and in the middle of it all, I disappeared. Like some sort of phantom, I was gone. The police radio crackled with my name being broadcast, and then, as if by some divine twist of fate, they found me. I was clinging to a lamp post, of all things, my feet pressed together whilst using an invisible hula-hoop. I have no idea how I had gotten there. The next day I learned that I was very close to the canal's edge, no barrier, no safety net, nothing to stop me from falling in. It was as if the universe had decided that I wasn't done yet. *"C'est la vie."*

I think back on it now, and somehow, that moment, that miraculous balance between life and death, feels like a symbol of everything that night meant. It was chaotic, dangerous, and very unpredictable, but it was also somehow perfect in its madness.

Magaluf

The ultimate preparation for a war zone, they called it. Five comrades, gathered for a week in a lovely apartment by the sea, the perfect backdrop for the kind of memories that make you laugh and cringe all at once. A place where we could embrace the madness, where every absurd decision became a part of our shared story. And, in a way, those days, wild and reckless as they were, taught us something that no military training could: the bond of true friendship, forged through chaos, and the understanding that, no matter how lost you feel, you're never truly alone.

In those carefree nights, we pushed our limits—dancing with reckless freedom, drowning in excesses of alcohol, and embracing the thrill of fleeting connections. Some of us found luck in love; others found it in the raw electricity of the moment. For me, it was both—a brief encounter with a warm-hearted northern lady who became my pen pal. Her letters, tender and thoughtful, were like lifelines during my time in Bosnia. Every fortnight, they arrived like clockwork, gently stroking my ego and lifting my spirits. Yet, despite her golden heart, I knew I wasn't ready for marriage.

As Bosnia loomed on the horizon, I threw myself into the challenge of becoming a door gunner. It began with a triumph: I became the first in course history to score a perfect 100% on the theory test. But the real test lay ahead in the practical—and what a test it was.

The Door Gunners Course was the epitome of adrenaline-fueled excitement. My most vivid memory? Firing tracer rounds at night, watching them streak like fiery arrows toward their targets below. Standing one foot boldly planted on the skid of the MK7 Lynx, grinning like a boy living out his wildest action-movie fantasies as the chopper banked and weaved through the air.

The sheer power of the GPMG (general purpose machine gun) in my hands was intoxicating, and I couldn't resist the primal urge to yell, *"Get some!"* as I peppered the ground targets with precision. It wasn't all fun and games, though. The course demanded intense concentration, especially when it came to mastering radio communications—a task that assessed my patience and skills more than anything else.

Then there were the ground drills: dismounting from the Lynx, moving swiftly over marshy terrain with the weight of the GPMG, and laying down covering fire as per the scenarios barked out by the DS. Each moment pushed us to the limits, sharpening both body and mind.

Though I dreamed of swapping my chaotic, fun haphazard days with MT Troop for the prestige and career prospects of aircrew, it wasn't meant to be. Still, the memories of that course remain a highlight of my service—a wild ride of skill, camaraderie, and a touch of sheer madness.

Bosnia

My memories of Bosnia are marked by extremes—the biting cold of high altitudes as we sat in the belly of a Hercules plane and the sweltering heat and oppressive humidity that greeted us on the ground. Each day felt like a collision of opposites, a land of both stunning landscapes and haunting reminders of conflict.

Our arrival at camp was met with an unforgettable scene that broke the tension of deployment: half-naked comrades gleefully launching themselves into a makeshift swimming pool. The pool, a 6x6 hole lined with plastic sheeting and filled from the fire-fighting water storage, was a masterpiece of resourcefulness.

Laughter echoed as uniforms were forgotten, and even officers weren't safe, thrown unceremoniously into the water by their grinning subordinates. It was a rare, beautiful moment of camaraderie, a reminder that even in the most austere conditions, we could create joy.

One of the camp's most critical duties was collecting stores and provisions from the NATO base in Split, Croatia. The job carried a unique blend of responsibility and danger. As part of the Air Corps, we had the distinct privilege—earned or otherwise—of removing our berets and issued combat tops while driving. It was a minor rebellion against uniformity, but one that made us feel just a little freer in a world bound by rules.

The road to Split was no casual drive. Navigating the treacherous mountain paths, often without crash barriers, demanded sharp focus. The rusted wreckage of vehicles scattered below the cliffs served as chilling reminders of the consequences of even a moment's lapse. But we pressed on, knowing the supplies we carried were vital to the camp's operations.

Monotony has a way of creeping in, even during the most perilous tasks. One day, leading a convoy of three trucks, I found myself growing restless. Spotting a civilian road worker as we passed, I couldn't resist the urge to inject a bit of mischief into the day—I sprayed him with my spare water.

The moment passed with a chuckle, and I continued to camp, blissfully unaware of the chaos I'd left in my wake. Upon arrival, I learned that my water-soaked victim hadn't taken the prank lightly. Furious, he'd retaliated by hurling a stone at the second truck, cracking its windscreen. My amusement quickly turned to sheepish regret as the consequences of my boredom became all too clear. *Oops,* indeed.

The drive to Split, a winding 3–4 hours of treacherous roads, carried a unique perk: an overnight stay on the NATO camp. These stopovers, far from being a chore, became the closest thing we had to a mini holiday—complete with camaraderie and indulgence.

After unloading provisions, the evening unfolded like a soldier's dream. First, a proper meal with our comrades, where laughter filled the air and toasts were raised. The pilots indulged in wine whilst us groundies and the (REME) Royal Electrical Mechanical Engineers, stuck to our trusty beer.

The night would often take us to a bar where we discovered *Kruškovac,* a pear liqueur that transformed into the most heavenly milkshake imaginable. Fuelled by good spirits and great company, we played games deep into the night before eventually piling into taxis back to camp. Located beside a serene lake, which became a haven for loud, boisterous British soldiers. Swimming under the stars, we embraced moments of pure joy, a fleeting escape from the weight of our mission.

On one such evening, my mischievous streak found its mark: a friend from basic training. Spotting his meticulously folded pile of designer clothes and pristine Lacoste shoes by the lake's edge, I couldn't resist. He never saw me coming, but the laughter—and his colourful language—echoed across the water.

Ours was a friendship forged in shared chaos and adventures, the kind that thrives in the unlikeliest of places. I still recall the time we found ourselves in Honduras, lured by a travel brochure's promise of idyllic beaches. What greeted us instead was a stretch of littered sand and a sinking realization that we were utterly lost.

Fate, however, had a funny way of intervening. We flagged down the only vehicle in sight—a beat-up pickup truck. The driver didn't speak a word of English, but he welcomed us aboard, beers in hand, as his three young children sat in the back with us. He was our guardian angel that day, guiding us out of nowhere and into the unknown, trusting strangers with his family in a way that left a lasting impression on me.

Bosnia, for all its camaraderie and resilience, held its darker truths. Near our camp, small stores selling counterfeit CDs popped up like weeds, strategically placed by the Mafia. Staffed by young women, their presence seemed legitimate at the time—a simple convenience. Years later, as a civilian, I came to understand the horrifying reality: these women were also victims of human trafficking, caught in a cruel web we were too naive to see.

The weight of Bosnia's tragedy deepened further when I learned of the horrors inflicted on Bosnian Muslim women during the war. The systematic brutality—Serbian soldiers using rape as a weapon of terror—was a haunting testament to the depths of human cruelty. It was a Holocaust in its own right, and its memory, like all atrocities, must never be forgotten.

Brac: A Taste of Paradise

Brac, a gem of an island nestled between Croatia and Italy, offered a blissful contrast to the intensity of Bosnia. Renowned for its warm climate, stunning views, and beaches straight out of postcards, it became a little slice of heaven during our tour. For three glorious nights, I found myself living the dream on the Army yacht, part of our much-needed R&R. Only five soldiers were allowed on the yacht at any one time, making it an exclusive retreat. The experience felt almost surreal—diving off the deck into crystal-clear waters, discovering the James Bond within me. We lounged in the sun, joked with mates, and admired the local scenery—not just the landscapes. For those few days, life felt uncomplicated, indulgent even. This was an Army lifestyle I could get used to.

Valika Kladusa

Valika Kladusa stands out as the cushiest posting I had during my time in Bosnia. Life there had a rhythm that felt too good to be true. Mornings began with a simple task: flushing the fuel bowser for twenty minutes, testing for sediment, and waiting for visiting aircraft. We frequently refuelled Czech Air Force Hip helicopters alongside our Lynx Mk7s, forging camaraderie with our allies across the airstrip.

I worked with a senior AAC soldier, who even taught me a few bass guitar chords during the downtime—a moment of mentorship and shared passion that made the posting even more memorable.

The routine allowed for a level of leisure I hadn't experienced before. I hit the gym three times a week and made regular trips to the library, which kept us stocked with the latest movie rentals. Meals were another highlight. The cookhouse served up a little slice of heaven every morning in the form of strawberry and banana omelettes. And then there were the local staff—stunning women whose smiles brightened every day. I grew especially friendly with one, but my inexperience meant my ambitions never quite took off. Timing, as they say, is everything.

The perks didn't stop there. A 24-hour canteen provided endless access to snacks and comforts. It was a far cry from the gritty reality of other postings. But the timing of my deployment played a crucial role. I was there during SFOR (Stabilization Force) when the mission was about maintaining peace. Had it been eight years earlier, during IFOR (Implementation Force), I might have been ducking bullets instead of enjoying banana omelettes.

The lazy soldiers often found humour in mocking the door gunners, laughing at how they had to lug the pilots' baggage. But every journey starts somewhere, and those who dared to dream of the skies knew that action paired with belief was the only way forward. Carrying bags wasn't a punishment—it was a stepping stone.

I find it inspiring to know that some of those very door gunners rose through the ranks to become pilots. It's proof that grit and focus on the destination can lead to incredible heights. To those who made it, kudos—you embody the spirit of perseverance.

The highlight of nastiness on my tour of Bosnia took place whilst serving the senior ranks at a makeshift dinner on camp in Gornji Vakuf. It was a moment that, at the time, seemed like nothing more than dark soldier humour, but in hindsight, it underscored just how troubled some of us really were—and why it's so important to treat our staff with respect.

I'll never forget the look of pure vengeance on his face. With words of hatred under his breath, he dropped his trousers, grabbed his tool, and proceeded to stir the alcohol before anointing the rim of his mug with the oozing pus from his bell-end.

At the time, it was just another outrageous stunt, a twisted form of barrack-room justice. But looking back, it speaks volumes about the resentment that can build when people feel disrespected and undervalued. Leadership isn't just about issuing orders—it's about how you treat those who serve under you.

Poland Exercise

Our first exercise after Bosnia was nothing short of unforgettable. The moment that stands out most vividly in my mind came during our off-duty hours. Out of nowhere, a woman appeared—dressed only in her underwear. She climbed onto a platform and began dancing provocatively, eventually giving the youngest soldier a private performance. It was a surreal scene; one I couldn't quite reconcile with the stark professionalism of our day-to-day duties.

651 Sqn sometimes trained alongside the Polish Air Force, blending our tactics and strategies in joint manoeuvres. But the work wasn't what made this exercise memorable—it was the Polish Officers' hospitality, a chaotic mix of tradition and mischief.

Invited to the Officers Mess, we found ourselves trapped in a ritual of relentless vodka toasts. Making eye contact with a Polish officer was like signing a contract—you weren't leaving until your shot

glass was filled, the toast was made, and the vodka burned its way down your throat. The sheer potency of the drink made my head spin, but the camaraderie in that room was intoxicating.

Of course, chaos was inevitable. One soldier disappeared into the woods naked and had to be tracked down. Another, known for his aggressive demeanour, crossed paths with someone tougher. The outcome? He returned with two black eyes and a bruised ego.

Our next exercise brought us to cross paths with the Americans, but I didn't realize this until one nerve-wracking night convoy. As the vehicle commander my focus was glued to the dim, 50p-sized light on the differential lock of the truck in front. It was our only guide in the pitch-black darkness, a fragile lifeline connecting each vehicle in the convoy.

Suddenly, a convoy of Abrams tanks roared past us. I was seated on the left side of the truck, and the tanks felt like hulking metal monsters emerging from the darkness. The ground shook with their passing, the deafening noise clawing at every nerve in my body. Every fibre of my being seemed to vibrate with the sheer power of those machines.

It was a frightening, humbling moment—a reminder of the raw, overwhelming strength of military machinery. I wouldn't be exaggerating to say I nearly shat myself. Moments like these are impossible to forget. They leave you shaken but alive, more aware than ever of the world that you're navigating.

Out of my comfort zone didn't even begin to describe it. As I cautiously edged my driver farther to the right, the unthinkable happened—our 8-tonne truck rolled over. "For crying out  loud!" Not just a little tip, but full-on barrel rolls, tumbling violently to the right. *"Bloody hell!"* I screamed as my heart pounded, adrenaline coursing through my veins. As surreal as it was, I couldn't help but love the rush. My driver, however, was far less amused.

Despite her semi-conscious state, she allegedly had the presence of mind to remember the drill: this was her golden ticket to freedom. While others scrambled to assist us—headlights cutting through the cold night and casting eerie shadows— my driver knew that this meant an escape from the freezing exercise, a flight to a warm hospital, and, most importantly, a well-earned cup of tea. I admire her ability to make the most of the situation, even if her sense of humour wasn't quite on par with mine in the moment.

25 Flight AAC - Belize

My six-month tour in Belize was nothing short of magical, aka the highlight of my AAC career. Ironically, I owe this experience to my MT Sergeant, a man I had sparred with on more than one occasion. With my B2 radio operator qualification and a knack for pushing boundaries, I became the only viable candidate. It was bravery—or sheer stupidity—that led me to get the last word with him one fateful day, eliciting a roar of laughter from the troop. Unfortunately for me, his laughter carried the greatest volume of all—he wrote my career reports, after all.

Once in Belize, I quickly realized I had landed in a world of wonder. As part of the AAC, we were tasked with casualty evacuations for infantry units training in the jungle for up to six weeks at a time.

New arrivals like me got a taste of jungle life immediately, spending a few nights immersed in its alien yet captivating rhythm.

The jungle's procedures fascinated me. Watching the resident instructing staff catch, kill, gut, and cook a jungle pig was a spectacle, and the meat? Unforgettable. I can still recall its smoky, succulent flavour, enhanced by the sheer primal satisfaction of the process.

Even the preparation of the oven felt like a lesson in ancient survival techniques. Rocks, heated to glowing red in a roaring bonfire, held their heat long enough to create a pit oven. The entire process was mesmerizing. Of course, the instructor eventually revealed a perfectly prepared tray of pig meat that had already been cooked, but the experience of learning the jungle method stayed with me—a vivid memory of ingenuity and simplicity.

The timing of my posting to Belize couldn't have been more perfect. The REME, made up the bulk of the adventurous training instructors, ensured we could squeeze every drop of excitement from our time there. Thanks to them, I learned to scuba dive and spent countless weekends navigating some of the most breathtaking dive sites imaginable—crystal-clear waters teeming with vibrant marine life, each dive like stepping into another world.

But the adventures didn't stop there. Jet skiing was another thrill I couldn't pass up, though it quickly proved to be one of the most physically demanding pursuits I'd ever tried. The sheer effort of staying balanced and controlling the machine left me sore but exhilarated, with a grin I couldn't wipe off my face.

The most memorable escapades were participating in caving expeditions into Guatemala. On one trip, we decided to stop overnight in San Ignacio, a charming little town nestled right on the border with Belize. The air was heavy with the scent of tropical blooms and a faint buzz of excitement as we pulled into town. It felt like the world itself was holding its breath for whatever would happen next.

By sheer chance—or perhaps fate—we arrived the very same evening as a group of lively American female students. The coincidence felt electric, like a match being struck in the dark, and before long, sparks were flying. Let's just say *WOW!* That night, the quiet town of San Ignacio came alive. The air thrummed with music, laughter, and just a touch of mischief.

As the night wore on and inhibitions gave way to the universal language of dance, it seemed there wasn't a single student left unaccompanied. Soldiers and students paired off in a way that felt both inevitable and utterly hilarious, aided no doubt by the generous flow of local beer and our well-fitted "beer goggles."

I thought I had taken a leaf from the Corps motto. I was asked if I felt the earth move. No! I replied with a big grin on my face. This was quickly removed, by her stating that there had been an earthquake during the night. The irony wasn't lost on us, and we laughed until tears streamed down our faces.

Texas

On my six-month tour of duty, we were given two weeks of R&R. Somehow, I managed to stretch this into three separate five-day holidays. One of these unforgettable breaks took me to Houston, Texas, where I reconnected with my US lady from San Ignacio.

She kicked off my trip with a visit to the Johnson Space Centre, a place that left me in awe of human ingenuity and exploration. That evening, we ventured into a trendy Latin Quarter neighbourhood for a meal with her friends. The vibe was electric—laughter, music, and the lively hum of the crowd made it feel like a scene straight out of a movie.

Another highlight was attending an American football game. While I couldn't fully wrap my head around the constant timeouts, the energy of the fans was infectious. Everywhere I looked, people raised their fingers in a horn gesture, shouting in unison as though it were a cult meeting. The camaraderie and passion in the air were unlike anything I'd experienced before.

But the true cherry on top came as a surprise. She revealed a pair of tickets to see Lenny Kravitz live at Southpark Meadows. The concert was nothing short of electric. With his guitar wailing under the Texas sky, I felt completely swept up in the moment, a perfect crescendo to an already unforgettable trip.

WOW! This woman must have truly adored me. That evening, after a few drinks, she hesitated at the thought of driving. Sensing her unease, I took the reins—because when life hands you a moment, you seize it. Moments later, we pulled into a parking lot just off the highway, swept up in the rush of adventure and connection. There, under the hum of passing traffic and humidity, we celebrated life with reckless pleasure.

The thrill of that evening didn't end there. As we merged back onto the highway, the familiar flash of red and blue lights appeared in my rearview mirror. A Texas highway patrolman had clocked us, and my heart pounded as the officer stepped towards my car. But fate had my back. The moment he realized I was a British soldier on vacation, we became fast friends. Whatever the breathalyser might have shown, he cheerfully waved me on, his demeanour suggesting he might have caught a glimpse of our spontaneous pit stop.

She wasn't just adventurous; she was a grounding force in my life. Coming from a wealthy family, she could have been aloof, but instead, she was kind and supportive. During my time stationed in remote places, she was my anchor to sanity, offering a warmth that reminded me of home.

Guatemala

When the chance arose to explore Mount Antigua in Guatemala with another soldier, I couldn't resist. The landscapes were nothing short of a dream—rolling greenery framed by the looming silhouette of an inactive volcano. Antigua itself was a picturesque gem, with its cobbled streets and a cozy café run by an English student who brewed the strongest coffee and served local dishes bursting with flavour.

Our group for the mountain hike included several women who brought an air of light-heartedness to the journey. As we ascended, we passed wild white horses grazing freely—a scene so idyllic it felt surreal. But the beauty was tempered by danger. The loose volcanic ash made footing treacherous, and the dense ash cloud often restricted our vision. Fate must have prevented us from stumbling into one of the steaming vents scattered along the trail.

That evening, as we celebrated our survival in a lively Guatemalan bar, I found myself drawn to a woman near the dance floor.

Though our words were few and halting, her smile and energy bridged the language barrier, yet I still got her phone number.

The next day, I decided to take a bus to Guatemala City. To my delight, she was true to her word, meeting me in the bustling heart of the city. The day felt like a reward for the risks of the hike and the spontaneity of my travels—a perfect ending to a whirlwind weekend.

Caye Caulker

My weekend in Caye Caulker with my Guatemalan girlfriend was like stepping into a postcard—a tiny tropical island reachable only by boat from Belize City. The crystal-clear waters, the laid-back atmosphere, and the warm breeze made it feel like a slice of paradise.

Our communication was comically modern for the time; the only way to stay in touch after our initial meeting was through faxes sent to 25 Flight AAC.

Her affectionate nickname for me, *"Sweet Pinocchio,"* often brought chuckles at work, but one REME soldier took the joke to the next level. He concocted a fake fax, claiming she'd met someone else and no longer wanted to see me. It was so well crafted that I couldn't help but laugh, and it provided a morale boost for the entire flight.

Caye Caulker was a favourite getaway for squaddies, and we often found ourselves sharing space with XXXL American tourists. The island was famous for its scuba diving, but we opted for snorkelling instead. The reef stretched far out into the turquoise waters, alive with vibrant fish and corals that felt out of this world.

Soldiers were forbidden from venturing into Belize City at night for our own safety—after dark, it became a haven for drug dealers and shady characters. But during the day, the town had its quirks, including the Amish community, who gathered around their store in their traditional attire, unchanged by the sweltering heat. They became a local attraction themselves, a curious contrast to the tropical setting.

Another evening on the island, I met up with a woman I'd first encountered while climbing Mount Antigua. We shared a lovely dinner, and she honoured me with her trust, revealing that I would be her first. What should have been a joyful and significant moment, however, turned into one of immense frustration for me—a novice faced with a situation I hadn't anticipated, faltering at the first hurdle.

It was a humbling experience, one that lingered in my mind as I sat under the night sky, listening to the waves gently lap against the shore. Belize had given me unforgettable memories of laughter, adventure, and connection, but it also left me with a sense of self-reflection, reminding me that growth often comes from the moments that challenge us most.

New Orleans

When I planned a weekend getaway to New Orleans, I thought it would be a chance to unwind with another AAC soldier from 25 Flt. However, an unwelcome addition to our group—a notorious thug from the permanent staff—changed the tone entirely. My unease grew the moment he stepped into the elevator with me at our hotel. As the doors closed, he turned the confined space into his personal boxing ring, using my stomach as a punch bag and landing a blow to my face.

I didn't retaliate, choosing restraint over rage, but I walked out with a bruised eye and an even deeper bruise to my spirit. The rest of the long weekend became a solo venture, navigating the vibrant streets of New Orleans with my black eye as an unwelcome companion. It was one of the most isolating and uncomfortable experiences of my life, a stark contrast to the city's liveliness.

Still, there were moments of solace. I tried New Orleans' famous Gumbo dish, its rich flavours providing a small comfort amidst the chaos. A visit to a tarot card reader offered me a glimpse of the city's mystical side, though I found little clarity for my current turmoil. I chose not to press charges against the thug. Instead, I held onto a quiet confidence that life has its way of balancing the scales. Some burdens are better left to karma.

Guatemala City

My next trip to Guatemala City was a chance to deepen my connection with my girlfriend and immerse myself in her world. Meeting her family was an experience filled with warmth and cultural discovery, but the highlight of my visit was an entirely different kind of plunge—bungee jumping off a bridge at night.

Initially, we had planned to jump in the afternoon, but the organizer's chaotic setup delayed everything until after dark. When I was asked to go first, I laughed nervously and deferred to another daredevil to play the role of guinea pig. Watching him take the plunge did little to calm my nerves, but when it was my turn, I stepped up, adrenaline coursing through me.

The first jump was electrifying. Standing on the edge of the bridge, I could no longer see the river below, only an endless void of darkness. As I leapt, my body tensed in freefall, every nerve screaming until the bungee cord finally retracted, jolting me upward with a wave of relief.

For my second jump, I expected to relive the thrill, but my body had other plans. Fatigued and over-adrenalized, I flopped off the platform like a sack of potatoes, the initial spark replaced by a mechanical sense of going through the motions. It felt anticlimactic, as though I'd already left my courage on the bridge with my first leap.

In hindsight, the second jump may not have been worth it, but the experience was unforgettable. It was a metaphorical leap of faith, much like my journey with my girlfriend—a blend of exhilaration, fear, and discovery, all wrapped up in the adventure of stepping into the unknown.

As the biggest adventure of my life drew closer to the end, I faced an awkward dilemma—I knew I wouldn't see this woman again, yet I didn't have the courage to tell her outright. Instead, I tried to ease into the inevitable goodbye by taking her out for a meal. But that evening, I was not my usual self.

That night at her home, the universe—or just the food— delivered its verdict. I woke up in the middle of the night, doubled over with food poisoning, and what followed was nothing short of apocalyptic. Projectile vomit sprayed everywhere, coating her shoe stand and seeping into her open wardrobe. It was a surreal moment: one part excruciating pain, another part uncontrollable laughter locked deep within me. If irony had a smell, it was right there in that room.

The chaos served as an unintentional escape hatch. Between the mess I had made and my queasy state, leaving her behind no longer felt complicated—it felt like survival.

Playa del Carmen

Playa del Carmen was a soothing interlude on my way to the vibrant nightlife of Cancun. I visited twice, each time savouring the slower pace and the postcard-perfect beaches. My second stay at a quirky little spot called Fawlty Towers B&B, I found myself in the middle of Thanksgiving festivities. I dined like royalty, surrounded by strangers who felt like family for one perfect evening.

There was a local girl I got to know during my visit. She was charming, and for a moment, I wondered if something might come of it. But as with so many of my fleeting encounters, nothing materialized. Instead, I left Playa del Carmen with fond memories of its idyllic sands and a promise to myself to return one day—this time with my wife, to share its magic anew. What a fantastic last memory to take with me home to Germany.

Iceland

Summer in Germany brought with it two weeks of unplanned leave, and after failing to rally the lads for a trip, I decided to take matters into my own hands. On a whim, I booked a flight to Reykjavik, Iceland. I'd read somewhere that its nightlife was among the best in the world, and though I had no plan, I was determined to find out for myself.

Arriving in Reykjavik, I quickly learned that Iceland wasn't cheap. My first night was spent in a cozy yet overpriced B&B, but I wasn't about to let my budget dampen my spirit. That evening, I ventured into a bar where I spotted other travellers—like me, they lacked the polished glamour of the locals, making them instantly approachable.

The city had an energy that was both wild and welcoming. Beneath the midnight sun, Reykjavik felt like a place where anything could happen—a perfect setting for a lone adventurer to stumble into unexpected friendships. It was a trip born of frustration, yet it became a testament to the magic of spontaneity.

It was a rare comfort to finally connect with people in a town that felt cold and distant. The streets carried an air of tension; locals often argued or even fought openly, adding to the unease. One evening, I ventured into a nightclub, hoping to find some sense of belonging, but the atmosphere was uninviting, even hostile. Desperate for a place to stay, I searched for budget options and stumbled upon the Salvation Army hostel. It was far from luxurious, but it was a haven—cheap, practical, and filled with fellow travellers seeking connection. In this small sanctuary, I began to form bonds that made the loneliness of the town fade.

One of my days took an unexpected turn when I knocked on a Canadian gent's door and was instead greeted by two Swedish girls with radiant smiles. It felt like I had stepped into a dream—I was in heaven! They, along with a Canadian traveller I met, made the days that followed feel alive with laughter and adventure.

Still, I couldn't help but feel a pang of envy for the organized travellers renting 4x4s, their freedom allowing them to experience nature in ways I couldn't. They had hours to take in the majestic landscapes, while my tour bus barely paused for thirty minutes. Yet, I made the most of my journey, including a rejuvenating visit to the Blue Lagoon. Its naturally heated pools enveloped me in warmth, and the mineral-rich mud, cool and thick, felt like a gift from the Earth itself. Again I thought to myself, "one day, I'll come back here with my wife."

Love Parade

There was barely time to catch my breath before I embarked on my next adventure—this time to the biggest rave in Europe. My excitement was electric, my heart pounding with anticipation. Armed with an Army sleeping bag slung over one shoulder and a 5ltr bottle of water in hand, I boarded the train to Berlin. With every stop closer to the city, more partygoers joined, their energy contagious. Big, silly grins and brightly coloured outfits filled the train, a prelude to the chaos of joy that awaited us.

When we finally arrived, the crowd spilled onto the streets, an unstoppable wave of revellers. I followed the flow for about twenty minutes, my steps fuelled by the pulsing anticipation that seemed to vibrate through the air. As Brandenburg Gate came into view, I stood in awe. Massive lorries adorned with speakers rolled past, each one pulling a float blasting music so loud it felt like the bass was shaking my bones. The Gate was alive—a kaleidoscope of colour, movement, and sound.

Amid the sea of dancers, I found my sanctuary—to the side where people were fully immersed in the music, lost in their own rhythm. The beats surged through me, and I surrendered to the euphoria of the moment. Hours passed like minutes, and I was a part of something greater, something beyond words—a collective celebration of life, freedom, and pure, unfiltered joy.

After a frenzied half-hour of raving in pure hardcore style, letting my pent-up excitement erupt onto the dance floor, I finally began to cool down. My heartbeat, still synchronized with the relentless bass, started to steady. That's when I caught her gaze—a Euro Babe with piercing eyes locked on me. Her look seemed to say, *"Hello, you fine-looking thing, why don't you come over here and dance with me?"* It would've been rude not to oblige her unspoken invitation.

As my favourite techno tracks pumped through the air, the bass pounding in my chest like a second heartbeat, I danced with freedom—like an overjoyed schoolboy on his first school outing. Her energy matched mine perfectly, and for the next 24 hours, I had the privilege of sharing my Berlin adventure with this gorgeous and captivating host. Together, we became part of the vibrant, pulsating spirit of the Love Parade—a memory etched forever in the grooves of my heart.

Australia

The seed for my Australian adventure was planted back in Belize, during a casual chat with a pilot who doubled as a hockey player for the regiment. Knowing my sporting abilities, he mentioned a hockey tour to Australia—a trip that immediately lit a fire inside me. The challenge? I had only six months to earn a spot on the squad. It wouldn't be easy, but the thought of representing my regiment down under was too tempting to pass up.

Thankfully, I wasn't starting from scratch. Having played as a reserve in my school team and being among the fittest in the regiment, I just needed to refine my skills—and, more importantly, stop barging into opponents like a bull in a china shop. The tournament welcomed players from all regiments on camp, and to my surprise, I ran into two more witnesses from boarding school who treated me with a warmth that felt surreal and welcoming that I had overcome bullying.

When July came, we touched down in Australia during their winter—a small blessing, as the cooler weather hid the gap between our abilities and theirs. Their team was stacked with talent, including an international, making every match a hard-fought lesson. But despite the steep competition, I earned the

"Most Improved Player" award, mastering the art of neutralizing their wingers without earning fouls. For a fleeting moment, I felt like I belonged among them, even as they outclassed us.

At the end of the tour, we were given time to explore. While some of my teammates opted for the sun-drenched beaches of the Gold Coast, I decided to embark on a scuba diving trip—a choice that, in hindsight, was a colossal mistake.

The dive site was a good two to three hours away from Queensland, but what I thought would be a breathtaking adventure turned into a nautical nightmare. The sea was rough—mercilessly so—and it didn't take long for the chaos to begin. One by one, passengers succumbed to seasickness. The sound of vomiting and diarrhoea filled the air, and before long, the toilet and cabin were utterly defiled walls and floors alike becoming unwilling victims. It was an unholy mess, and I couldn't escape the misery.

By the time we reached the reef, my stomach felt like it had been wrung dry, but I stubbornly suited up for the dive. Beneath the waves, the beauty of the underwater world should have captivated me, but the pain in my ears quickly overpowered any sense of wonder. My ego begged me to push through, but after only ten minutes or, I had to admit defeat.

When the boat finally docked, I felt a surge of relief so strong it was almost spiritual. A fellow diver and I both dropped to our knees and kissed the ground like shipwreck survivors returning to land. Exhausted, battered, and thoroughly over it, I could think of nothing else but finding my bed and escaping this ordeal.

Germany

As my Army career progressed, I found myself yearning for something more—a path that offered both purpose and better prospects. The solution seemed clear: transferring to the REME as an Air Tech. The wages were higher, the promotion opportunities plentiful, and the work more aligned with what I wanted for my future. I approached the REME OC, a man who also coached the rugby squad and had always treated me with kindness. He listened, supported my plan, and set the wheels in motion. Now, all I had to do was wait for the transfer exam papers to arrive.

But amidst this period of transition, something happened that I hadn't anticipated—a moment that stopped me cold. Whilst on base, I noticed a uniform displaying a surname that made my stomach drop. It was the name of the boy who had taken advantage of me, a name I could never forget. I froze, my heart racing as I tried to process what I was seeing.

From 100-200 yards away, I studied him. He was taller than the boy in my memory, and I realized that it must be his younger brother. Still, the sight of that name sent a jolt through me, and for a moment, I was transfixed, unsure whether to confront or flee.

But then, something remarkable happened. I didn't react impulsively. I didn't let the emotions overwhelm me. Instead, I stood there, breathing, grounded in the knowledge that I was stronger now—stronger than the pain, the fear, and the ghosts of the past. That moment became a powerful symbol for me: proof that I had overcome the bullying and the adversity that once held me down. This was my final witness to my growth, my resilience, and my capacity to take back control of my life.

Germany was a wild chapter in my life, filled with camaraderie, chaos, and those small yet significant moments that shape who you are. It was messy, it was beautiful, and it was unforgettable.

Norway

In September 2000, I overheard some of the lads at the bar swapping plans about a three-month adventure, skiing, and partying across Europe. They made it sound like a dream come true, and I was in before they could finish their pints. *"Sign me up, mate!"* Fitness wasn't an issue—I was already part of the regiment's rugby and hockey teams—and I even had a bit of skiing experience from a previous trip to Bavaria with 651 Squadron. All I needed was to connect with the regimental ski rep, who, true to form, was found tearing up the slopes.

A Captain from RHQ took charge of organizing everything with military precision and delegating driving duties among the team. Before long, we were packed and on the road to Norway.

The thrill of travel buzzed in my veins—I've always loved the excitement of the unknown, of not knowing who or what might be waiting just around the corner. Spirits were high as we imagined the picturesque landscapes and, let's be honest, the Norwegian ladies we were bound to meet was an exciting prospect.

We arrived just as the sky was darkening, the air crisp with the promise of winter. That first night, we kept it simple, heading to a local bar near our accommodation. It wasn't long before one of the senior lads showed his generous side, buying round after round of beer for the group. The atmosphere was lively, made all the better by the stunning blonde barmaid who clearly caught his eye. By the end of the night, it was clear she was going to be his companion for the trip—a match sparked by a shared smile across the bar.

The next morning, we hit the slopes for our first day of skiing. I was eager to get my skis back on, but overconfidence has its price. I went down hard—*spectacularly hard*—in a crash that drew applause and laughter from the team.

That evening at dinner, I was ceremoniously awarded a leopard-print chef's hat for 'Best Crash of the Day," an honour I accepted with a mix of pride and sheepishness.

After dinner, we decided to fuel up properly for the evening ahead. We found a cozy restaurant, where plates of hearty food helped us prepare for what would inevitably be a night of debauchery. With

our stomachs lined, we followed the pulsing beat of drums and the hypnotic flash of skylights to a nearby club.

The club was alive—a sanctuary of music, energy, and possibility. As soon as we walked in, we made a beeline for the dance floor, letting the rhythm loosen the stiffness from a day on the slopes. It wasn't long before I left the group to scope out the scene, wandering the club in search of like-minded ladies who might be open to a bit of fun and flirtation.

The air buzzed with the mingling scents of cologne and beer, the lights casting a kaleidoscope of colours across faces flushed with laughter. It was the kind of night where anything felt possible, where the lines between strangers blurred, and connections—no matter how fleeting—felt electric.

Norway had only just begun, but already, it was shaping up to be an unforgettable blend of adventure, camaraderie, and wild nights under the northern skies.

Amazingly, I managed to share a taxi home with a captivating lady from the club—a spark of excitement to end an already memorable night. But as we crossed the threshold into my cabin, the atmosphere shifted. She seemed restless, as though something had suddenly changed. The cold air on the journey had sobered her up, bringing clarity to her thoughts. Or she'd received one of those silent, vibrating text messages that signal an urgent call home. Then again, it might have been me—

fidgeting awkwardly, suddenly more aware of my own sobriety and lacking a clear plan of action.

Whatever the reason, her mood couldn't be salvaged, and before long, she was gone. The evening ended not as I'd hoped, but as I sat alone in my cabin, I am reminded that 'life is all about choices.'

The next day was that defining day!

The most outrageous experience of my Army career happened whilst I was detailed as the Regimental duty driver. It all began with chaos—a rushed handover from someone with admin worse than mine. I barely had time to process the predicament before being tasked to collect an officer from a neighbouring town for a court martial at PRB.

The journey to pick him up was uneventful, though my anxiety was contained. The officer, a composed and almost serene figure, entered the vehicle, and we merged onto the autobahn. That's when he gently shattered my illusion of competence: *"Driver, we're heading in the opposite direction."*

Wake up, Laing! My stomach sank as I realized my mistake. Apologizing profusely and sweating like I'd run a marathon,

I prepared to turn off the next exit for the direction of PRB. But fate—or my neglect—had more in store. My worst nightmare came true: the Land Rover sputtered and finally stopped. Out of fuel.

To make matters worse, the only jerry can onboard was empty. I froze, my thoughts racing with self-recriminations and dread over what disciplinary actions awaited me.

The officer must have been an angel, as without a word of reproach, he jogged into the horizon, disappearing into an unseen destination. Minutes felt like hours, but true to his miraculous nature, he returned within ten minutes, carrying a full jerry can of fuel.

The least I could do was take over refuelling. My hands trembled as I sheepishly completed the task, then drove back to the court martial with the officer, his demeanour unchanged. To this day, the aftermath remains a blur. Not a charge, not a rebuke. Instead, I walked away unscathed, my reputation bruised but my record intact. It wasn't skill or foresight that saved me that day—it was sheer, undeserved luck.

In the Army, I was often called a 'Jammy Git' aka someone who possessed extraordinary, irritatingly good fortune. Others may chalk it up to coincidence, but looking back, I sometimes wonder if my enlistment wasn't about serving my country, but God's inexplicable sense of humour to improve morale.

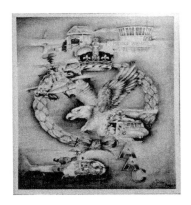

This was drawn by Cpl Al Finlay, who at the time was posted to RHQ AAC as clerk for AGC (Adjutant General's Corps)

Printed in Dunstable, United Kingdom

65775127R00070